Competent
Counsel

Competent Counsel

WORKING WITH LAWYERS

Denise G. Shekerjian

DODD, MEAD & COMPANY
NEW YORK

To Michael Metz

The sample attorney-client agreement on page 111 is reprinted by permission of The National Resource Center for Consumers of Legal Services.

Published by Dodd, Mead & Company, Inc.
79 Madison Avenue, New York, N.Y. 10016

Distributed in Canada by
McClelland and Stewart Limited, Toronto

Manufactured in the United States of America

Designed by Jeremiah B. Lighter

2 3 4 5 6 7 8 9 10

Library of Congress Cataloging in Publication Data

Shekerjian, Denise G.
Competent counsel.

Includes index.
1. Attorney and client—United States. 2. Lawyers—United States. I. Title.
KF311.S523 1985 340'.023'73 85-1646
ISBN 0-396-08696-9

Contents

Preface

FOR MOTIVATED people, day-to-day living can get complicated. If you are interested in writing a will, setting up a trust, buying or selling a piece of property, getting married or divorced, adopting a child, starting or selling a business, finding your way through a maze of government regulations, signing an important contract, forming or dissolving a corporation, entering into a partnership, fighting a tax investigation, or making some critical investments, the chances are that you will need a lawyer. And not just any lawyer, but a smart one who will take the time to understand your goals and protect your interests.

The purpose of this book is to help you obtain solid legal advice at a price you can afford. The initial chapters discuss how to decide if you can manage without a lawyer, when to seek help, whether to choose a generalist or a specialist, whether you need a large firm or a small firm, and how to work with the attorney you hire. You will also learn what you can legitimately expect from your lawyer and what he or she will expect from you, how to make the most of your relationship, and how to evaluate performance and hold him accountable for what he promises to do. The important subject of cost is covered as well. A good attorney is expensive, but not nearly as expensive as a bad one. You will learn how a lawyer sets fees, how to read and dispute bills, and how to trim charges for the services you desire. And just in case things don't go according to plan, you will also learn how to discharge an attorney if you need to, how to bring him up on charges before the disciplinary committee, and if the situation is really serious, how to sue for malpractice.

Just ten years ago, finding a competent lawyer who could serve your needs was no simple task. Lawyer advertising was taboo, an attorney who held himself out as a specialist was asking for trouble from the local bar association, and the neighborhood legal clinic was thought to be an experiment that wouldn't pan out. And lawyers themselves didn't help matters much: standard operating procedures included minimal communication with clients, unitemized bills, and price fixing. (The latter used to be completely legal for attorneys but a serious violation of the antitrust laws for any other businessman.) Happily for the consumer of legal services, times have changed.

Some key Supreme Court decisions, abolishing minimum fee schedules and lifting the ban on lawyer advertising, signaled the start of a transition from a profession that purported to police itself to one shaped to an increasing degree by the demands of the marketplace. As a result, low-cost clinics and prepaid group legal plans are springing up all over the country. In some places, you can get legal advice over the telephone and charge it on a credit card. Specialization is also on the rise as is advertising, and indeed, wholesale merchandising campaigns. The number of law firms that have retained a public relations consultant has more than doubled in the past year. Even stuffy Wall Street firms are putting out impressive brochures to attract new clients. The consumer of legal services is better informed and therefore more powerful than ever before.

Coupled with the increase in information is the fact that the supply of lawyers is out of step with demand. Consider some statistics compiled by Barbara Curran, Associate Executive Director of the American Bar Foundation. In 1960, the number of lawyers in this country totaled roughly 250,000, which worked out to 1 lawyer for every 632 persons. By 1970, the number of lawyers swelled to approximately 334,000, or 1 lawyer for every 572 persons. By 1980, the ranks of lawyers had grown to half a million—that's 1 lawyer for every 418 persons. It is estimated that in 1990 this country will be swamped with 1 million lawyers.

These figures are staggering. What it means to lawyers is that most of us are headed for some tough times. To be prosperous, a lawyer will not only have to master a specific and timely speciality but have to become an expert in marketing as well. What it means to you, however, is that quality will go up, costs will go down, and the sophisticated consumer will enjoy opportunity and leverage as never before.

❖

Acknowledgments

THE WRITING OF this book profited immeasurably from the assistance of many people. My warmest thanks and gratitude:

To the staff at the American Bar Association and the American Bar Foundation for their able assistance with the research of this book. I am also very appreciative of the many people affiliated with state and local bar associations across the nation who provided me with information;

To Charles Stillman, Julian Friedman, and Edward M. Shaw, three skilled attorneys from whom I learned a good deal about the proper practice of law;

To the staff at Dodd, Mead & Co., Cynthia Vartan, my discerning editor, and Alexandria Hatcher, my capable advisor; and finally,

To my parents, and to Karen Colvard, James Fessenden, and Michael Metz, friends to whom I am deeply indebted for their ideas, comments, and encouragement.

Competent
Counsel

CHAPTER ONE

Is a Lawyer Really Necessary?

SOME OF THE OLDER brethren at the bar remember when the public held the legal profession in the highest esteem. That was a time when a lawyer occupied a place of moral authority in the community. His opinion on just about anything (including the law) was courted and, in some circles, revered. Then came Watergate. The resignation of President Nixon under threat of impeachment, the disbarment of his closest advisors, and the imprisonment of former Attorney General John Mitchell took a serious toll on the public's perception of lawyers. An annual Louis Harris & Associates poll conducted during these years, for example, repeatedly cited a greater amount of public confidence in trash collectors than in law firms.

Although a profound distrust has been generated by the acts of only a few prominent lawyers, the remainder of the bar is not free from blame. It is not difficult to pinpoint the areas of public discontent. At the top of the list is the ubiquitous question of money. The commonly shared perception is that lawyers make too much and clients are left with too little. It is not unusual in metropolitan areas, for example, to hear of fees in excess of $280 per hour. Summer interns at Wall Street firms are raking in a whopping $900 a week, not to mention a princely bonus upon acceptance of the job, and perks such as theater tickets, chartered boat cruises, catered picnics at Shakespeare in the Park, golf outings, and evenings on the town, all courtesy of the firm. That's a very sweet deal for second-year law students, who haven't even finished school let alone passed the bar examination.

There are other grievances, too. It seems that the smallest matter, when handed over to a lawyer, becomes a lot of fuss and bother. Clients are often kept in the dark. Paperwork is generated in a language that purports to be English but, without a translation, might as well be Greek. Despite an appointment fixed weeks in advance, a client can be kept waiting for hours. Moreover, when something truly urgent crops up, the receptionist informs you that your attorney is either in conference, out of town, away from his desk, or all of the above.

These among other annoyances justify the conclusion that if you *can* do without a lawyer, you *should.* Unfortunately, however, most legal problems are too complicated to chance to your own devices. You are not without alternatives, though, and these should be explored before you commit yourself to the task of finding an attorney you can afford and with whom you can be comfortable.

HELP FROM NONLEGAL PROFESSIONALS

Not every problem that raises legal considerations requires the assistance of a lawyer for its resolution. Quite a lot of information can be obtained from other professionals with whom you may deal. Prominent among these are accountants, bankers, and realtors. Each of their fields skirts and at times overlaps the turf of the legal profession. If your problem falls within the expertise of any of these persons, it is worth your while to make an appointment to discuss your situation. You are certainly free to disregard the advice you receive, and in most cases, it costs you nothing to inquire.

Accountants: A good accountant can provide valuable tax advice and some basic financial planning for your personal needs, family or business. He or she should be able to assess your financial situation and help you to frame your short-term and long-range investment objectives. An accountant can also review the prospectus or offering plan of a venture you are thinking of putting money into and help you to determine the risks. One of the most valuable services an accountant offers, however, is his ability to save you money. Versed in the Internal Revenue Code and up on the latest rules and regulations of the current administration, a capable accountant can make a tremendous difference to your lifestyle. Unless the Internal Revenue Service has alerted you to an ominous problem or investigation—in which case you should immediately seek the advice of a tax lawyer—an accountant is a good person to go to for help in solving your financial problems.

Bankers: Another source for financial planning is the trust department of your bank. If you are looking for tax shelters or want to set some money aside for the future, a banker can supply you with a variety of alternatives. While not authorized to draft legal documents to structure your estate, a banker can acquaint you with the issues and help you to frame your financial objectives.

Realtors: If your concerns involve the buying or selling of a home or undeveloped property, residential or commercial leases, zoning problems, easements, deeds, title problems, or the like, add a local realtor to the list of persons to speak with before you reach a decision as to the necessity of counsel. A good realtor has a respectable command of real property law, and while he or she is prohibited from the actual practice of law (unless the realtor is also a licensed attorney, which is increasingly common), you might be able to gain a lot of legal information about the transaction you seek to accomplish. The details of financing arrangements, title insurance, and closing procedures are within the sphere of information you can gain from a realtor. Moreover, in some states, the realtor is empowered to draft the contract of sale. Be wary, however, of an overly eager agent. If he or she is interested in preparing a deed, mortgage papers, or accompanying affidavits and security agreements, you should be certain to ascertain that your state authorizes the realtor to act in this capacity, for it is usually the exclusive domain of a lawyer.

The accountant, the banker, and the realtor are all of potential value to you, but before you speak with any of them, two points of caution require your consideration. The first is that each of these professionals brings a particular perspective to your situation and each, to varying degrees, has his or her own interests to promote. The banker would be delighted to invest your money for you, but is he offering a suitable form of investment at the best rate available given your circumstances? The realtor would be most accommodating when it comes to structuring your land deals, but is he or she overstepping the permissible boundaries of law? By all means, go ahead and talk with these experts, but if you decide to use their services in lieu of a lawyer, be certain you are clear on what you stand to gain and lose.

The second and more obvious caveat is that since you are not dealing with licensed attorneys, you should not be seeking legal advice from any of these professionals, or assume that you are protected, legally speaking, should you decide to follow the course of action outlined for you. If your transactions or questions happen to fall squarely within their operating sphere, you may be fortunate to be able to avoid the trouble and costs involved in hiring an attorney. If not, beware of the temptation to regard the "substitute" as the real thing.

INFORMATION AVAILABLE TO YOU FOR LITTLE OR NO COST

Happily, there is an abundance of free or nearly free information available to you for the asking. Since in this age, information is power, it makes a lot of sense to exhaust these resources before you reach any decisions about hiring a lawyer. Despite the compelling logic of this approach, it is remarkable how few people take the time to check into the available options. Even if it is ultimately determined that none of these organizations can solve your problem, your conversations with these various agencies will at least assist you in framing the issues.

There are an increasing number of private foundations and government agencies that provide free information upon request. The effectiveness of these organizations varies, depending on funding and staffing, but even in the most inefficient bureaucracies, there is likely to be *someone* who knows what he is doing. Consider what a phone call can accomplish:

- *Business:* If your questions concern business, there are a number of resources available to you. Legal questions about the structure of the business (e.g., articles of incorporation, certificates of doing business, bylaws, taxation, filing requirements, name changes, and partnership agreements) may be addressed to the office of the corporation counsel for your state.

  If your question is more in the nature of deciding upon

business strategy, you need to speak with an experienced advisor. Springing up in increasing numbers these days are volunteer advisory groups made up of retired executives, who would be pleased to meet with you to discuss your business venture, point out its shortcomings, and steer you onto a smoother course. While the services of some of these groups are free, others charge a nominal amount as a consultation fee, usually ranging from ten to twenty-five dollars for one half hour. In addition to a face-to-face consultation, some groups offer helpful pamphlets and educational video tapes on various subjects such as how to incorporate, what to do when you need to fire an employee, how to seek financing, how to read a financial statement, how to find new markets, and similar matters. Two such organizations in New York City, for example, are the Executive Volunteer Corporation [415 Madison Avenue, New York, New York 10017; (212) 566-0214] and the American Woman's Economic Development Corporation [60 East 42d Street, New York, New York 10165; (800) 442-AWED in New York State; (800) 222-AWED elsewhere]. A third organization that is nationally based is SCORE, or Service Corps of Retired Executives (26 Federal Plaza, Room 3130, New York, New York 10278, (212) 264-4507). If this approach interests you, call your community board for a listing of the organizations available in your area. Your state's Department of Commerce, Office of Economic Development, or chapter of the Small Business Administration (SBA) also should be able to provide you with lists of sources of information and publications for the small business.

The Small Business Administration's Office of Management Assistance has a wealth of information in its own right. The SBA distributes close to ten million books and pamphlets a year at no cost or at a nominal charge. There are close to two hundred titles to choose from, covering subjects such as how to start a business, financial business management, marketing, writing a business plan, hiring and firing employees, accounting, inventory control, and many others. They even offer complete plans, called the "Starting Out Series," which address specific types of businesses. To order a catalog of their publications, write: SBA Publications, P.O. Box 15434, Fort Worth, Texas 76119. Ask for SBA Order #115A for a list of their free publications and SBA Order #115B for a list of publications sold at a nominal charge.

- *Civil Rights:* If your problem is one of discrimination or what you perceive as a violation of your civil rights, try speaking with someone at the American Civil Liberties Union, the Equal Employment Opportunity Office, the National Organization for Women, or the National Association for the Advancement of Colored People. See what they can do for you before you conclude that you need to go elsewhere.

- *Consumer Protection:* If you have a consumer complaint or question, your local Consumer Protection Board, Consumer Credit Counseling Service, Consumer Product Safety Commission, or Department of Consumer Affairs may have information on solving the difficulty. Privately funded consumer groups might also be willing to assist you with your problem. Check the yellow pages for listings, or phone your local civic organization and ask them for a roster of public interest organizations in your area.

- *Courts:* If what you need is help understanding the operation of the court system, when and where you are supposed to appear in court, what papers are to be filed in connection with a court proceeding, and other such matters, speak to the court clerk. He or she is most often located in the courthouse itself. Have all the necessary papers in front of you before you call, and bear in mind that clerks are not inclined to discuss anything at length. It will help if you are patient and persistent.

- *Environmental Concerns:* Environmental problems such as complaints about air or noise pollution should be addressed to the Environmental Protection Agency or Board.
- *Family Relations:* If your problem falls in the area of family relations or child care, contact your local chapter of the city's Family Services Agency or Family Services Board. If they can't help you, they may be able to refer you to a community group that is equipped to address your situation.
- *Health:* Health questions are properly addressed to the health and/or human services department of your local government. If you do not obtain satisfaction on this level, speak to the state equivalent of this office.
- *Insurance:* If you have an insurance question, a phone call to the State Insurance Commission or the local representative of this office may help. If your insurance concerns relate to benefit packages, you should also try the Department of Labor, Division of Employment.
- *Licenses:* If your question falls in the area of licenses and permits, a call to the state licensing board may be helpful.
- *Real Estate:* If you have a zoning question, call your local zoning board or town council. You can learn what the law is at present, how it affects your property, and what steps need be taken to register a complaint or to file for reconsideration.

If your question concerns improvements to property or restoration of an older building, it is advisable to look into the restrictions on changes imposed by your town or city before you undertake the expense of an alteration. Call your local housing authority, landmarks preservation committee, buildings department, or property board, and ask them to send you a copy of the regulations that apply to your circumstance.

- *Social Services:* If yours is a welfare problem, try contacting your town's welfare board or the Department of Social Services.

  Social security questions may be answerable by the social security office. If they can't be specific enough for you, try calling the Department of Social Services and ask to speak with someone versed in this area of the law.

- *Taxes:* Even the Internal Revenue Service has an information number if you have questions about your tax return or taxation in general. The IRS will also answer many specific questions addressed to them in writing and issue what's called a "private letter ruling." These rulings are limited to questions where there is confusion about the taxation laws. The IRS will not answer questions which concern factual issues. (For example, if you have a question about the deductions available to you, write the IRS; if you want to know the value of property you own, the IRS can't help you.) The IRS answers roughly forty thousand of these inquiries a year. To obtain a written ruling, write: IRS, Associate Chief Counsel (Technical), Attn: CC:IND:S, Room 6545, 1111 Constitution Avenue, N.W., Washington, D.C. 20224. Include the pertinent background to your situation or transaction, the question you want answered, and your name and address. If the response you receive rules against you, a copy of this letter must be attached to your tax return. Finally, while the phone and letter service are free, you may prefer to seek out someone other than Uncle Sam for tax advice.

Every town, city, and state labels its services and agencies differently. In trying to locate any of these resources, consult the front of your phone book, where "community service numbers" are often listed. If this does not prove fruitful in your location, consult the white (or blue) pages under the heading "United States Government" if you are trying to reach a federal agency or the name of the town for local services (for example, "Harvey Cedars, Boro of"). The yellow pages may also be helpful under the heading "Social Service Organizations."

Finally, if you are unsure of whom you should call with your question or problem, ask your Community Board, Community Council, Board of Aldermen, Office of the Borough President, or a librarian. Incidentally, a good librarian is invaluable.

SELF-HELP

If consultation with nonlegal professionals and the advice you gain from government agencies and citizen groups do not suffice to dispose of your problem, another alternative you should consider is to solve the problem on your own. Self-help, while hardly a new concept to the American justice system, is gaining in popularity these days. As far as the legal system is concerned, rest assured that in all but a handful of situations you have a constitutional right to proceed *pro se*—that is, on your own behalf. While you are certainly authorized to proceed without counsel, however, the more pertinent inquiry is, should you? The pros and cons should be carefully evaluated by asking the following questions:

1. How complicated is your situation?
2. How much will it cost you to do your own work?
3. Are you able to perceive your own best interests?
4. How grave are the consequences of making a mistake?
5. What resources do you have at your disposal?
6. What resources are at the disposal of your opponent?

A truthful answer to these questions will help you to determine if it is safe to take yourself on as a client.

How complicated is your situation? If all you seek to accomplish is to beat a traffic ticket or collect a security deposit, it is likely that with a little effort, you can succeed on your own. Both traffic court and small claims court are completely manageable forums for the layperson. Other problems may not be so simple to tackle. If your interest is filing for a divorce or writing a will, for example, the law can be a lot more complex. If there are no children involved and if the property at issue is not consequential, it is conceivable that with careful perseverance, you will be able to obtain your goals without the benefit of an attorney. You should recognize, however, that there are serious risks involved and no guarantees that everything will go according to plan. While an attorney may have no difficulty accomplishing your objectives, he or she knows how to avoid the pitfalls and skirt the traps. That's advice that is worth paying for and that can save you heartache in the long run.

How much will it cost you to do your own work? Certain fees are unavoidable even if you elect to handle your affairs yourself. There are, for example, docket fees associated with most court appearances, forms to buy, filing fees when you register a deed or process corporation, partnership, or litigation papers, notary costs, and other expenses whether or not an attorney is involved.

There is also the question of whether you know enough about the law to take full advantage of it. Ignorance can be costly. And let's not forget your time for all of this. If all that is required is an hour or so to fill in the right blanks on the right form—certainly, your time is a cost worth absorbing to avoid legal fees. If it will take you several days and a lot of running around to accomplish your objective, you might ask yourself whether it is worth the price. You may well conclude that your time is more valuable than a lawyer's.

Are you able to perceive your own best interests? There are some problems in life that involve one emotionally, and this has a tendency to cloud one's better judgment. Separations, divorce, child custody battles, estates and trust work, and serious personal injury cases present situations that draw one in so close that it may no longer be possible to remain detached and level-headed. In these and similar circumstances, it can be very helpful to have an attorney on board. He or she not only will represent your interests but can act as a mediator and a cool head when emotions run high. If you think you can benefit from having an objective, buffering influence around, it may be in your best interests to retain an attorney. When tempers flare, you will be well served to have someone on your side both representing your views *and* thinking clearly.

How grave are the consequences of making a mistake? Before you decide to represent your own interests, every effort should be made to ascertain the gravity of the consequences if you make a mistake or lose the battle. In some circumstances, such as the drafting and filing of articles of incorporation for a new business, mistakes as to content can be remedied with ease by filing an amendment. Other mistakes may not be so simple to correct. An error in the witnessing of a will, for example, could be enough to invalidate the entire document, which means that the disposition of your assets would be handled according to state law irrespective of your last wishes. Similarly, if losing a court battle simply exposes you to a modest fine, you may well conclude that payment of the fine is cheaper and easier than hiring a lawyer. On the other hand, if an adverse decision exposes you to harsh financial penalties, censure, the establishment of a record, or loss of liberty, you would be foolish to run the risks.

What resources do you have at your disposal? The uncertainty involved in doing your own legal work requires that you err on the conservative side when it comes to assessing ability and resources. Certainly time, intelligence, and perseverance are necessary at a minimum to cut a path through the legal jungle. If you are lacking in any of these resources, chances are you won't be happy with the results you achieve. As far as time and perseverance go, either you have it or you don't. When it comes to intelligence, however, help may be available. Happily, a growing collection of how-to books and kits is emerging to guide the layperson through the maze of our legal system. Some of the more popular titles include:

The Writer's Legal Guide by Tad Crawford (New York: Hawthorn, 1977)
Do You Need a Lawyer? by Philip J. Hermann (Englewood Cliffs, N.J.: Prentice-Hall, 1980)
How to Be Your Own Lawyer (Sometimes) by Walter L. Kantrowitz and Howard Eisenberg (New York: Perigee, 1979)
The Women's Guide to Legal Rights by Jane S. Lynch and Sara L. Smith (Chicago: Contemporary Books, 1979)
How to Avoid Lawyers by Edward Siegel (New York: Fawcett Crest Books, 1979)

Before You See a Lawyer: An Everyday Guide to the Law by Robert Weber (Piscataway, N.J.: New Century Publications, 1981)

In addition, many state bar associations (see the Appendix) also provide valuable self-help literature on various subjects as does the Nolo Press (950 Parker Street, Berkeley, California 94710 (415) 549-1976), which offers excellent books such as *Bankruptcy: Do It Yourself, How to Change Your Name, How to Do Your Own Divorce, Small Time Operator—Managing a Small Business, Author Law, The Partnership Book, Everybody's Guide to Small Claims Court,* and more. The Nolo Press materials are very well written and tremendously useful. Another helpful source is the American Entrepreneurs Association (90954 Worldway Center, Los Angeles, California 90009), which sells relatively inexpensive self-help kits to guide the layperson through the incorporation of a business.

A trip to your library and bookstore is mandatory to determine if a resource guide covering your area of interest exists. Note the date of publication and steer away from anything that is not fairly current. As a rule of thumb, the absence of a good commercial "how-to" guide is a sure clue that you had best seek legal assistance.

What resources are at the disposal of your opponent? If your problem is not adversarial in nature, you can disregard this question. If you do have an opponent, however, and that person has hired a lawyer, you would be foolish not to do the same. No matter how thoroughly you prepare and how capable you believe yourself to be, a layperson is no match for a seasoned lawyer. The odds favor experience.

A WORD OF CAUTION

If you have weighed the pros and cons and are still determined to have a go at it on your own, there are a few guidelines to keep in mind. First, while it is perfectly legal to fly solo, it is imperative that you confine your efforts to your own problems. Though your confidence may be bolstered at the success you obtain on your behalf, you cannot perform the same service for any other person or corporation, with or without compensation. To do so would constitute a crime: practicing law without a license.

The second thing to remember is that the law is fluid. What is gospel today may be overturned tomorrow; what is true in one state may not be true across state lines; procedures in one city may be completely different the next town over; what applies in one case may not apply in yours; one judge's preference is another's pet peeve. To compensate for what appears to be a rather arbitrary system of justice, your best bet is to double-check all your assumptions and information with a second source such as one of the resources mentioned earlier. While there is still risk involved (the second source may be less knowledgeable than the first), at least you have attempted to minimize the likelihood of error.

The third important point of caution concerns the mistaken assumption of many self-helpers that they will receive special consideration if a mistake is made. This is completely untrue; there are no breaks for the inexperienced. You will be charged with having full knowledge of the law as well as of the rules and regulations of the court. If you are blessed with good fortune, your mistakes may go unnoticed, but they certainly will not be excused on grounds of ignorance.

Finally, if at any time you feel that you are floundering, do not hesitate to seek help. It's never too late to hire an attorney, and an intelligent person knows when to cut his losses. At least you can take heart in the fact that your efforts at self-education will not be wasted; they will prove invaluable to you when it comes to working with the attorney you hire.

❖

CHAPTER TWO

Taking Stock

HIRING a professional person is not a process smart people take lightly. It's a safe bet that you wouldn't randomly pluck a surgeon's name out of the yellow pages. Your attorney should be selected with equal care. Like every investment in your future, it takes time and energy to bring about the right result. The payoff is almost always worth the effort.

By now, you have reached a decision as to whether or not your problem can be solved without resorting to the help of a lawyer. If you have concluded that the advice of an attorney is what's needed, the next thing to do is to get organized. Take a few moments to size up your situation. The important questions are: When should you consult a lawyer? Should you look for a specialist or a generalist? Do variations in style of practice really make a difference? What size firm is best able to handle your affairs?

WHEN TO CONSULT AN ATTORNEY

If a lawyer must be consulted, the best time to do so is before you are desperate for help. Early consultation allows you to get to know each other and establish a rapport. It's nice to have your attorney interested in you or your business before you have to rely on him. Familiarity with his style and confidence in his ability will save you time and reduce worries. With your working relationship in place, you can depend on getting results.

In the early stages of any venture or potential difficulty, your options are more numerous than at any other time. This flexibility affords your attorney the leeway necessary to structure the best arrangement possible under the circumstances. Moreover, if you face serious difficulties or litigation, early consultation is vital to reaching a resolution before your situation matures into a full-fledged headache.

There is also an economic advantage to early consultation, which should not be underestimated. Contrary to popular belief, costs for legal services are sharply reduced, in most cases, by bringing in a professional early on. It's basic dollars and cents that the more compounded your problem—aggravated during the time you put off going to an attorney in the hope that if you closed your eyes, it would go away—the more expensive its resolution. Also, the more quickly you have to have results, the more you should expect to pay.

The time to get in touch with an attorney is when you first learn that you have a problem. There are of course hundreds of problems or circumstances that could prompt you to seek help, but in general, you should get in touch with an attorney if you face any of the following situations: You are buying or selling a business; you are involved in a divorce or separation; you are sued or wish to sue; you are buying or selling real estate; you have sustained serious bodily injury; you are bankrupt or have severe credit problems; you have persistent and aggravated difficulties associated with your employment; you face immigration or naturalization problems; you are about to commit a significant amount of money or assets in a venture that is outside your normal course of dealing; you are making or signing important documents that affect property or personal rights (such as a will, trust documents, an important contract, or a deed); you are served with a subpoena; you are arrested; you are charged with a crime; or you are the target of an investigation.

GENERAL PRACTITIONER OR SPECIALIST

One decision you will have to make early on in your search is whether you require the services of a generalist or a specialist. A general practitioner is one whose practice is varied but confined to the common problems or needs associated with everyday life. An uncomplicated will or trust, the buying or selling of a home, a simple divorce, a contract or partnership agreement, the incorporation of a small business, simple tax advice, a personal injury claim, and occasional court appearances are a few examples of the kind of practice a generalist thrives on. As a rule, generalists can handle themselves pretty well when it comes to routine, garden variety situations.

There is something about the generalist that holds a special appeal. His or her balanced view of things, unpretentious service, and ability to solve a wide number of common legal ailments are deserving of the most profound respect. In many ways, the generalist is similar to a family doctor. Each comes to know you and your family through the years, helps you to grow strong and be secure, knows your objectives, sees you through your disappointments and enjoys a permanent place in the fabric of your life. It is with some sadness that one sees the generalist, like the country doctor, becoming a thing of the past.

Replacing the generalist is the specialist whose emergence is the inevitable by-product of a number of factors. Prominent among these is the observation that there is simply entirely too much knowledge for any one person to absorb and master in the law. The historic view that anyone who graduates from law school is capable of handling any legal problem is simply not so. Even the most brilliant mind is no match for the sheer volume of material that comprises our system of laws. A lawyer who wants to be successful must consciously delineate an area of practice according to interest, aptitude, and desired income.

Another force contributing to the tide of specialization is the fear among the legal community that branching out beyond one's expertise exposes a lawyer to malpractice suits. If an attorney takes on a case that is outside his usual sphere of practice and the client is unhappy with the results, the lawyer stands a very good chance of being sued. Whether or not the client is successful in his malpractice claim, simply the institution of the suit itself is enough to tarnish a hard-earned reputation and cause insurance premiums to rise. In this litigious society, a lawyer has no choice but to define clearly an area of practice and be scrupulously cautious about the kind of case he or she takes on.

Adding fuel to the movement is the fact that specialization can be extremely lucrative, particularly if the attorney masters a complicated area such as securities work, mergers and acquisitions, litigation, taxation, patent and trademark law, bankruptcy, admiralty, antitrust work, labor law, or computer law, to name a few. As one quickly gathers from this litany, these are fields that address the needs of large and rich clients with big problems—people who have a lot of assets to protect and propagate. A seasoned expert can enjoy a long and profitable future with just a couple of good accounts.

Roughly ten years or so ago, there was a heated exchange among bar members as to the desirability of imposing formal rules on attorneys who wished to claim an area of specialization. The proponents argued that a formal system of recognition and regulation would assure the public that one who claims to possess a particular skill is indeed competent in that area. The opponents countered with arguments about how specialization would splinter and factionalize an otherwise united fraternity of lawyers. They pointed out that our law schools are not set up to promote specialized knowledge and that the older practitioners would be handicapped by new educational requirements and tests designed to weed out those whose skills had atrophied over time. There was also sharp discussion over whether specialization would promote tunnel vision, which in the long run would be a disservice to clients.

While the desirability of specialization is still at issue in some circles today, the real debate now concerns how it should be implemented and regulated. It is an issue that you, a consumer of legal services, should be acquainted with because it clearly affects your decision making.

In 1979, the American Bar Association (ABA) came out with its Model Plan for Specialization, which set forth the minimum standards to be met before an attorney could claim to possess a speciality. The plan addressed factors such as the degree of involvement in a particular field, the length of time and percentage of practice in the area, the amount of advanced education obtained, and the desirability of a review by a peer board before an applicant could lay claim to the status of a specialist. In addition to the model plan, the ABA devised specific standards for twenty-seven fields of law.

The model plan served as a discussion paper for each of the state bar associations. Drawing upon its principles, a few states have adopted certification requirements for specialists, which consist of a combination of advanced training, a minimum number of years of practice in the field, and some form of oral or written examination. California, for example, has a specific set of certification standards for an attorney who wishes to specialize in criminal law, family law, taxation, or workers' compensation. Other states that have certified specialization programs are Arizona, Florida, Georgia, Iowa, Louisiana, Michigan, Missouri, New Jersey, New Mexico, Rhode Island, South Carolina, Texas, and Utah.

These stringent measures for certification are far more desirable than the rules adopted by other states that simply provide for the "designation" or "recognition" of a speciality. Designation or recognition allows an attorney to enter the marketplace as a specialist without having to complete any rigorous testing requirements. As such, it is difficult for the consumer to know to what extent the attorney limits his practice to this area, whether the attorney really does possess a true expertise, or whether he or she simply would like to attract more business in the areas designated as so-called specialities. Some states, such as Florida, have both designation and certification options.

The lesson in this is simply that if you are thinking of hiring a specialist, it is imperative that you call your local or state bar association (see the Appendix) to determine what requirements, if any, the state imposes before you conclude that the attorney really must be an expert. While a handful of states have abandoned or vetoed efforts to devise specialization standards, the majority are at varying stages in the formulation of rules. Until the profession as a whole takes steps to standardize formal recognition of the specialists, however, the consumer cannot rest secure in the claim of professed expertise.

With the trend toward specialists firmly entrenched, it behooves you to take a closer look at the advantages and disadvantages of using one. In theory anyway, a specialist assures a higher degree of competence and quality. There is nothing startling about this—the more you do something, the better you get. He or she has done a countless number of the same types of transactions over and over again and is familiar with every nuance, subtlety, and gradation. As for cost, you will probably come out even with the generalist. While the specialist usually charges a higher rate for his services, his proficiency allows him to handle the work in a fraction of the time it takes a generalist, who must first educate himself in a new field. On the other hand, the specialist is most often capable of handling very few and specific areas of the law. If your problem develops into another area, you may find yourself having to pay two lawyers, not one.

So which do you choose? If your needs are well defined and limited to a single purpose (such as buying a house, drafting a will or trust, setting up a business, securing tax advice, or solving family problems), opt for the specialist on the assumption that he or she will save you a great deal of time, money, and mistakes. If you aren't sure what your needs are, however, then start with the generalist and explain your situation. Be sure to ask him or her if you would be better off with a specialist. An honest lawyer won't hesitate to give you a truthful answer even though it means losing your business for the time being.

If a specialist is what you need, the next question is, what kind? Before it was disbanded, the American Bar Association Standing Committee on Law Lists compiled a roster of 158 areas of specialization. As might be expected from a list this lengthy, it reflected a considerable range of human activity. While commonplace subjects such as corporate law, insurance, commercial transactions, estate planning, family practice, and the like were covered, the list went on to cite an eclectic array of disciplines including drainage and levee law, chancery practice, livestock law, motion picture law, nuclear law, federal gas law, shopping center law, space law, steamship law, timber law, aircraft title law, and cemetery law.

The problem with 158 and counting specialities is that a client in search of an expert is faced with entirely too much choice. If all you want is a will, it is clear, of course, that you don't need anyone versed in space law. While it is a simple process to rule out the more esoteric disciplines, however, you must still decide whether to search for an estate planner, a family law practitioner, a tax expert, a lawyer who concentrates in probate, or a general practitioner. Similarly, if you are audited and serious omissions from your tax return are uncovered, do you face an IRS investigation, a civil or criminal tax problem, litigation, a criminal perjury charge, or all four?

It's not always easy to pigeonhole your needs. To help you along, here is a list of common transactions and the type of specialist capable of handling each:

- If you require a will or trust documents, want to dispute a will, need to probate an estate, seek to avoid probate or simply need help in sorting out your financial objectives, tailor your search for an estates and trust lawyer.
- If you want to buy or sell commercial or residential property including a house, cooperative, or condominium; clear title to property or establish boundaries and water rights; or negotiate, break, or challenge a lease, look for a real estate lawyer.
- If you want to set up a business, draft corporation papers, form or dissolve a partnership or corporation, want to enter into a contract of some significance, need help in deciphering a prospectus, or are interested in making an investment in a business or commercial undertaking, you need a corporate lawyer.

- If you have been injured, are being sued or want to sue as a result of an injury, or need help in processing or contesting a personal injury claim, you should look for a personal injury lawyer. If your injury is the result of a defective product, you should consider retaining either a personal injury lawyer or a products liability lawyer.
- If you want to file a personal or business tax return, shelter income, donate funds to charity, restructure your estate to benefit your children or spouse or other selected individuals, or better understand the deductions available to you, tailor your search for a tax lawyer.
- If you seek to copyright your work or obtain a patent, defend a trademark, or prevent disclosure of a trade secret, you need a copyright and patent lawyer, sometimes referred to as a patent and trademark attorney. In the area of trade secrets, you might also consider speaking with a corporate or labor lawyer.
- If you are the subject of employment discrimination, have troubles with your union, are seeking to defeat the election of a union, or want to prevent unfair competition, you need the services of a labor lawyer.
- If you are bankrupt or in the red, creditors are persistent and you want to schedule your debts, or an involuntary bankruptcy proceeding has been filed against you, you need a bankruptcy lawyer.
- If you want to file for divorce or separation; are asked to sign a prenuptial contract; are seeking alimony, palimony, or child support, or want to adopt a child or name a guardian for one, you need a domestic relations lawyer.
- If you are arrested (even if you are innocent), served with notice of an investigation commenced against you, served

with notice that you are to act as a key witness in a criminal proceeding, believe you are being watched or your calls monitored, or notified that you are to appear before a grand jury, you should immediately call a criminal lawyer.

- Finally, if you are being sued or want to sue and your problem does not fit into any of the above categories, contact a litigator. If a more specialized skill is needed, the litigator can advise you on the type of specialist who handles your need.

While the above list is by no means exhaustive, it should serve to steer you in the right direction.

STYLE OF PRACTICE

An attorney's particular expertise is not the beginning and end of your inquiry. Equally worthy of consideration but more difficult to pin down is the question of the attorney's style of practice. The way in which an attorney approaches his work can be decisive in delicate situations. Many a good claim or defense has gone down the drain simply because the attorney adopted the wrong approach, an offensive tone of voice, or an inappropriate manner. While style is personal and individual, some generalizations can be made to illustrate this point.

Negotiators: Some lawyers are excellent negotiators. They have an aptitude for sorting out and evaluating competing interests and know how to bring about a skillful settlement. Successful negotiators are talented mediators and even better listeners. They have an instinctive understanding of give and take yet at the same time are shrewd enough to know when to cut their losses. They know how and when to bluff, when to remain poker-faced, and the right time to show a little courage. If negotiation can be applied to your circumstances to stave off costly litigation, it is worth your extra effort to find a first-rate lawyer who possesses this strength. Unless you have dollars to burn, it is almost always better to settle the mess than to hash it out in court. Even where questions of principle are involved, if you can strike a compromise you can live with, so much the better.

Noisemakers: In contrast to the negotiator, some lawyers can best be characterized as noisemakers. Their strength is in making their presence known. Troubles with a customer who ignores his bills, a cleaners with whom you've failed to communicate, or an irritable landlord who won't take you seriously are problems that can demonstrate the prime utility of a noisemaker. A brisk letter on his or her stationery followed by a phone call will make it amply clear that you request your due and will not tolerate any further nonsense.

Noisemakers, if brought into a problem early enough, can be very effective and inexpensive. One word of caution, however: Noisemakers should be retained only for small or very small concerns. Serious risks deserve serious attention. It is a grave mistake to give the impression that you are ready to take action when in fact you are unwilling or unable to do so.

Technicians: Some legal needs require less talking and more doing. If you require concrete services such as tax advice, the drafting of contracts or wills, the structuring of corporate documents, assistance with government regulations, and a variety of other generally nonadversarial concerns, neither the negotiator nor the noisemaker will do you much good. What is required under these circumstances is a well-educated, well-versed technician. The right person for you is the one who reads all those new releases that clutter up most lawyers' desks, someone who gets excited by detail and is a fanatic for precision. The technician's greatest strength is in knowing his or her product inside out. He may not be the most personable or polished speaker in the world, but when it comes to actually thinking through and cranking out the paperwork, a person with technical skills is the one you should insist on.

Clerks: Certain problems are not so complex that they require someone as skilled as the technician described above. Indeed, many legal problems simply require a lawyer to fill in the right blanks on the right form within the time limits imposed by law. Such routine problems do not require any great or novel thinking, complicated strategy, or sophisticated negotiating. Either the form is filled out properly or it's not. For these kinds of problems, you would be best off with what I refer to as a legal clerk—a lawyer who knows where the forms are and who can select the right one, fill it in properly, mail it to the right place or stand in line and be done with the whole affair in a timely fashion. There is nothing inherently bewildering about the process, and you don't need to pay top dollar to solve the problem.

Advocates: Finally, if you are faced with a problem that will bring you into litigation, you cannot afford to hire anyone less than the best advocate your budget can afford. No matter how complex or cut-and-dried your issues appear, litigation is costly, time-consuming, unpredictable, and aggravating. Not every lawyer's predilection, it requires a particular disposition and a lot of trial experience to be successful.

The person for the job is someone who not only knows the system but thrives on cutting through it. The advocate enjoys public speaking, revels in the challenge of a volatile situation, is attracted to the limelight, and exudes a certain savvy, charisma, and winsomeness. He or she has to perform well and think quickly under pressure. Strategy and rhetoric should be second nature. It also helps if your advocate looks polished and speaks with conviction, as the weak and timid are often discounted. In many ways, trial work can be likened to public theater. If thoroughly prepared and well executed, it is dramatic, eloquent, and persuasive. It doesn't take too many mistakes, however, to ruin the whole performance. Advocacy is tricky and exhausting—if you need it, look for an old hand who thrives on it.

THE SIZE OF THE FIRM

There are roughly forty thousand law firms in the United States at present, ranging from the sole practitioner, in business for himself, to national and international giants boasting in excess of six hundred attorneys. In view of the possibilities, some thought should be given to the size of the firm best able to handle your needs. The pros and cons of the three basic sizes—small, medium, and large—outlined below should guide you into making the proper selection for your needs. Size considerations notwithstanding, however, your decision should ultimately rest on the actual attorney who will be handling your case. If the person is bright, competent, experienced, and responsive, the size of the firm with which he or she is affiliated should be of secondary importance.

Small firms: For purposes of discussion, I consider a small firm to possess between one and five lawyers. There is a plentiful supply of law firms in this range. Indeed, recently compiled statistics by the American Bar Foundation report that roughly half the lawyers engaged in private practice in the United States are sole practitioners. And sole practitioners coupled with two- or three-person law firms constitute roughly two-thirds of the private lawyer population.

At times, a sole practitioner will affiliate himself with other sole practitioners or a small law firm in the interest of sharing common expenses and cutting overhead. Though the solo attorney may share facilities with other lawyers, it is incorrect to assume that he or she is a *member* of that firm. Don't let the presence of a handful of lawyers fool you into thinking that you are dealing with a single firm when in fact it may be a collection of firms operating under the same roof. Each firm has its own responsibilities and obligations (both to its members and to its clients) and is not responsible for any other firm unless there is an express understanding to the contrary.

There are some significant advantages to a small firm. Foremost among these is the fact that prices are often lower because there is less overhead. It is also likely that your case will receive a great deal of personal attention and care. Fewer lawyers usually results in greater accountability.

While these advantages may appeal to you, if your demands are time-consuming or unusually complicated, you may want to think twice about a small firm. The greatest danger in a firm this size is that they will accept a case that they are unable to handle. Oftentimes the little guy does not possess the office staff or library necessary to gear up for a protracted battle or intricate negotiation. Where litigation is concerned, for example, resources can make or break your case. Similarly, if your problem requires a composite of different skills, a small firm or a solo lawyer simply may not possess the expertise in-house.

There is the question of time as well. All firms have other clients, of course, but in a small firm, a bustling practice can put you at a distinct disadvantage. When your lawyer is busy looking out for the interests of other clients, who is minding yours? Similarly, can you afford a delay if your lawyer suddenly becomes ill or an emergency requires him to close up shop for a while?

Large firms: On the other side of the spectrum are the megafirms, also known as the law factories, assembly lines, sweatshops, and paper mills. Fifteen years ago only a handful of firms had as many as one hundred lawyers. Today, in major urban areas, this is considered modest. Moreover, a look at law firm development in recent years prompts one to conclude that big is vogue. Consider, for example, Finley, Kumble, Wagner, Heine, Underberg, Manley & Casey. In 1968, they had all of eight lawyers. Today, they have over four hundred with offices in eight cities, and they are still growing.

While sizes vary, in my book any firm that sports over one hundred lawyers is a large firm. There are a number of advantages and disadvantages to a firm this size. Let's first consider the bright side.

Large and, indeed, monstrously large firms have tremendous resources at their fingertips. Their staff support can include a sea of secretarial help as well as battalions of clerks, paralegals, messengers, receptionists, and office administrators. Some even have full-time economists and environmentalists; others bring in special lecturers to conduct seminars on topics of interest to their clients.

In addition to ample staffing, the research facilities can be awesome. Not only are large firms likely to have full-sized libraries, but their collection is frequently computerized and managed by one or more librarians who keep things in order and expedite research requests. Elaborate file systems of research memoranda and so-called "brief banks" are likely to be maintained, greatly reducing a lawyer's need to start from scratch in solving a given problem. Many large firms are also subscribers to a computer research service (such as Lexis or Westlaw), which is an expensive but valuable time-saving tool. (While services vary, most allow instant access to all federal and state cases and statutes; an international trade library; over 150 news and periodical sources; federal agency regulations;

company and industry financial reports; tax, patent, accounting, and admiralty libraries; the laws of select European countries, scholarly publications, and a government document file.) All these resources, available twenty-four hours a day, seven days a week, 365 days a year, can deposit a wealth of information on a lawyer's desk.

In addition to their staggering resources, large firms can lay claim to a number of specialities, each of which is finely honed and presumably state-of-the-art. Without exception, large firms are formally compartmentalized into separate legal disciplines sometimes referred to as "boutiques." One bunch of lawyers just handles real estate, for example, another dozen or so are corporate experts, a handful specialize in insurance matters, the excitable ones are litigators, and so forth. This variety of expertise under one roof can work to a client's advantage where the legal need is particularly intricate. For example, if a corporate lawyer, working on the establishment of a business, runs into intricate tax considerations, he can just phone his neighbor in the tax department a few offices down and does not need to waste valuable time either educating himself or calling around outside the firm for help. The superlarge firms carry this concept of "full legal services" even further by making available their affiliated offices nationwide or worldwide.

Large firms also possess the advantage of lots of extra hands, which assures continuity of representation. The illness, vacation, or emergency of a lawyer can be accommodated by bringing one of his or her partners up to speed on the matter. There is always a way to share the work load in a large firm.

Another important feature of the large firm is the deep pocket. A large firm is more likely to remain solvent (a problem in recent years) and assume financial responsibility in the event of a malpractice claim. While in ideal worlds, you should never have to call upon a firm's insurance coverage, it is a comfort to know that the recourse is available should the need arise.

Despite all the wonders a large firm has to offer, however, there are some distinct disadvantages you should consider. To begin with, all that overhead costs money to sustain, which means that the client more often than not is paying top dollar. If your problems are severe or the stakes high, it may be worth your while to pay a premium for well-experienced specialists and tremendous resources. A part of every bill, however, includes the costs associated with maintaining an ambience of success and power.

For all their manpower, another drawback you should consider is the fact that a large firm may not be as responsive or as capable as you would like. Responsiveness and quality of service depend upon the actual attorney who is handling the matter. While on the basis of your interview of the firm you may conclude that the partner you spoke with is able and competent to handle your affairs, he or she may not be the attorney who will be actually managing your case.

The work load in a large firm is assigned within each department according to the degree of experience and available time the attorneys have. The sale of your modest property holdings, for example, would most likely be relegated to the newer, less experienced associates in the real estate division while the more capable senior partners concentrate on handling the meatier matters likely to go on for some time and result in repeat business. When a lawyer sizes up a new matter, he does so in terms of billable hours. It is a fact of lawyering that the bigger your problem (translation: large quantities of billable hours), the more high-caliber attention your case will receive. While there are always exceptions, this is particularly true in the colossal firms. They operate on a dollars-and-cents basis. Their concern, first and foremost, is the bottom line. The more you have to offer them, the more responsive they are apt to be.

Another disadvantage to the large firm is that it usually caters to big business and not to the everyday living of everyday people. As such, big firms specialize in corporate work, complex litigation, antitrust matters, commercial real estate, sophisticated taxation, estates and trusts work, and other similarly lucrative fields. The concerns of the paltry individual or closely held mom-and-pop businesses are of marginal if any interest to them.

Medium-sized firms: In between the two extremes of David and Goliath lies the medium-sized firm, which for purposes of discussion I will assume is composed of anywhere from 6 to 100 lawyers. Within this range, my admitted bias is for the firm with less than 30 lawyers. In the usual case, firms of this size are relatively new to the marketplace (five to fifteen years old) and haven't been around long enough to experience the growing pains of their giant-sized compatriots.

Often composed of younger lawyers who are anxious to make a name for themselves in an overcrowded profession, these firms will usually give the attention required to a smaller client. Their reputation is not so secure that they can afford a less than fully committed effort. Responsiveness means repeat business, and they know it. Moreover, new clients may not be banging down their door, so they depend upon a kind word from you at your next social gathering for their incoming cases. If you are interested in a firm that will take the time to know you and grow with you, your family, or your business, investigate the low end of the medium-sized firms.

Another advantage to medium-sized firms (and particularly the newer, smaller ones) is that they often possess a variety of skills that interact in a way that a large, rigidly compartmentalized firm cannot (or does not) provide. The members of a younger firm are still friendly and informal enough to talk with each other. It is not uncommon, for example, for the lawyers to meet on a monthly basis simply to bring each other up to date on their caseloads and to share opinions and suggestions as to how to handle difficult problems. (In a large firm, the lawyers of one department may not meet the other members of the firm until the annual dinner dance or firm picnic.) This teamwork is sensible, productive, and to your benefit. It is a fine atmosphere for treating all sides of your situation.

Another benefit of the smaller, younger firm is that they usually do not have such high salary expectations or overhead as the big firms and are likely to pass the savings on to you. Their address is not as prestigious; they do not have oil paintings of the deceased-but-still-omnipotent partners lining the halls; they do without plush carpets, lovingly polished oak conference tables, and graceful spiral staircases joining their many floors. There are no brass nameplates on office doors, no subsidized dining halls, no uniformed messengers, and they get by with one computer instead of a terminal on every desk. All these extras, designed to obtain the cutting edge on quality, attract clients, and impress adversaries, are costly to clients. As a general rule, the less fancy the firm, the more palatable the bill.

On the con side of the equation, the midrange firms have less staff and smaller research facilities at their disposal. In addition, they do not have affiliate offices strung across the globe and are not likely to be equipped to handle the concerns of big business. If you feel that your case will require these resources, your decision is made. If your work is more routine, however, there is a greater likelihood of your being satisfied in a smaller firm than a larger one.

CLINICS

An alternative to a traditional law firm—the law clinic—has taken hold with more or less permanent roots. While clinics have been around for roughly twenty years now, their recent popularity can be attributed to a number of causes including the fact that while a veritable tidal wave of graduating lawyers floods the marketplace each year, law firm openings are few and very far between.

Apart from a lack of jobs, however, is a heightened sensitivity to the fact that the delivery of legal services in this country is sadly deficient with respect to low- or middle-income families. People who are too rich to qualify for legal aid and too poor to afford the hourly rates around town—70 percent of our population—are forced to consider legal services as a luxury which cannot be satisfied before other more pressing needs are met. The elderly, handicapped, persons of moderate means, students, and artists are among those in need of an alternative. The middle class is a virtually untapped market, and many lawyers have begun to devise ways of capturing its business.

Perhaps the most cataclysmic events giving rise to the growth in legal clinics, however, were two Supreme Court rulings, which have dramatically altered the fabric of legal services in this country. The first of these opinions occurred in 1975 in a case named *Goldfarb v. Virginia State Bar.* In *Goldfarb,* a Virginia couple lost patience with the fact that every lawyer in their area adhered to a "minimum fee schedule," which dictated the lowest dollar amount lawyers could charge for a given service: they were unable to find a lawyer who was willing to charge less than $522.50 to assist them in the purchase of a home. The exasperated couple sued the Fairfax County Bar Association on grounds that the minimum fee schedule violated the Sherman Antitrust Act and exerted a restraint on commerce. The Supreme Court wholeheartedly agreed. Until this decision, it had been the common practice in all jurisdictions for bar associations to issue "minimum fee schedules." The schedules were used both to satisfy a lawyer that he wasn't underselling his services as well as to defend his fee against disgruntled clients. The Supreme Court ruling now prohibits the legal profession, like any other profession, from fixing prices.

The second important opinion that changed the complexion of the delivery of legal services occurred two years later in a 1977 case named *Bates v. State Bar of Arizona.* Here, two Arizona lawyers were censured for an advertisement they placed in the local paper describing some of the services and costs their firm had to offer. They appealed the censure to the Supreme Court, which decided that state laws and bar association rules prohibiting lawyer advertising were in conflict with the constitutional right to free speech. As a result, lawyers are now permitted to advertise (within limits) the availability of their services, costs, location, expertise, and similar information. State and local bar associations still retain authority to impose some restraints, however, but there is a constant battle over where the First Amendment leaves off and permissible regulation begins.

These two cases have ushered in a new age of deregulation in the legal profession. The result is that legal services now operate in closer accord with the principles of a free market system—that is, consumers are better able to make an informed choice about the products and services available to them. The green light on competitive fees and advertisements not only expands the market but redistributes the business to those who advertise and offer the lowest rates.

As might be expected, these changes were not welcomed with open arms by many established members of the bar. Advertising was considered offensive to the notion that the proper way to establish a practice was the way Abraham Lincoln did it—by building a solid reputation. Furthermore, the die-hard traditionalists claimed that the Supreme Court rulings would promote commercial, vulgar, and unprofessional behavior. (And in truth, Richard Greene, writing for *Forbes* magazine, reports that we now find some law firms offering discount coupons, employing press agents, and placing ads on matchbook covers and bowling alley score sheets.) The essence of professionalism, the opponents claimed, is service to society; earning a living is supposed to be a secondary and incidental consideration. In short, there was a lot of resistance and regret over what was perceived to be a transformation of the craftsman into a businessman.

What was not said but, it is fair to assume, was lurking near the heart of at least some of such objections was that the high court rulings promised to cut into a lawyer's profits. Minimum fee schedules and the absence of advertising produced artificially high rates, since price competition was close to nonexistent. The Supreme Court paved the way for alternatives, and the clinics seized the opportunity. Whereas in 1974 there were eight known legal clinics, today there are hundreds with perhaps the oldest among them, Jacoby & Meyers, still going strong.

Opinions vary as to what a legal clinic is, and no single definition has yet emerged. There is agreement, however, on the hallmarks that characterize a clinic and distinguish it from a conventional law firm: a high volume of business; low costs at fixed rates according to published fee schedules or written quotations; service to low- or moderate-income clientele; efficient and streamlined operations; reliance on standard forms, paralegals, and word processing; convenient locations in shopping centers or on the main thoroughfare; easy payment terms; convenient hours including evening hours; and a strong dependence on advertising. As one quickly gathers from the foregoing, the idea is essentially this: By limiting services to only routine cases, keeping costs at a minimum, and attracting a high volume of clients through advertising, competent and reliable service can be achieved at very competitive prices.

There are advantages and disadvantages with a clinic that should be considered before electing to hire one in lieu of a traditional law firm. With respect to the advantages, clearly the most salient one is cost. Almost all clinics are competitive with other prices around town, and more often than not, they charge less than the prevailing rates. There's no magic to how they do it. By accepting only the most routine cases and relying on paralegals and standardized forms, the expensive advice of a lawyer is obviated and the savings are passed on to you. Of course lawyers are available, but if you don't need one, why pay those rates?

Another advantage, clearly, is that legal clinics are accessible. Not only are they located in highly traveled areas such as shopping centers with evening hours, but the consumer is more likely to hear of the existence of a clinic through advertisements. According to a 1980 survey conducted by the National Resource Center, the average annual advertisement budget of a clinic was $8000, which worked out to be roughly $8 of fees generated for every $1 of advertising. The most common place for advertising is the yellow pages, followed by local newspapers. The more prosperous clinics have turned to radio and television. With all this coverage, accessibility is guaranteed.

Two California lawyers have carried the notion of accessibility one step further by opening a variant on the law clinic called The Law Store. With branches in Montgomery Ward outlets among other places, The Law Store allows a client to walk in without an appointment, pay the cashier ten dollars, enter a phone booth, and obtain a direct line to a staff lawyer. If this is still too much trouble, The Law Store offers a toll-free number that you can dial from home, and they will put their legal charges on your credit card.

A third advantage to clinics is that their initial consultations are usually quite informative. If your problem or case is not one that the clinic can handle, you are more likely to receive information as to where to go and how to proceed during a clinic consultation than at a law firm. Indeed, over 60 percent of the clinics surveyed by the National Resource Center indicated that the promotion of self-help was one of their main services. This is partly because most clinics have a philosophical interest in improving the availability of legal services (which means educating the public whenever possible) and partly because they have standardized methods for dealing with the cases they refuse as well as the ones they accept.

While the clinic has a lot to offer, there are some distinct disadvantages you should be aware of before you decide to retain one. The first is that the clinical practice is by necessity limited to run-of-the-mill, uncomplicated cases. If your needs do not fit neatly into the streamlined, standardized systems and forms set up to handle these types of cases, you are in the wrong place. Clinics cannot afford to give a case individual attention at the low rates they charge. Your initial consultation should establish if your problem fits the mold. If your matter is not routine and the clinic accepts the case anyway, chances are you won't be saving any money because the fixed rates will not apply. You might also question whether the clinic is capable of handling anything outside the norm.

The composition of a clinic's practice varies from place to place. The two biggest areas of concentration are divorce matters and bankruptcy. Other services, however, may include wills, trusts, separations, support, custody, adoptions, real estate, driving while intoxicated (and other minor criminal matters such as shoplifting), corporate documents, name changes, evictions, traffic offenses, probate, basic contract law, workmen's compensation, landlord and tenant disputes, small claims, personal injury cases, consumer complaints, and immigration.

A second problem with legal clinics is that the quality of the service can vary tremendously. The same is true in law firms, of course, but you shouldn't conclude that just because a clinic has standardized its operations, the handling of the cases is consistently correct.

If the disadvantages are not enough to deter you, there is one thing to keep in mind when shopping around. Not every organization that calls itself a clinic is one in fact. If the group you talk with is offering more or less traditional services at the going rate and does not appear to be employing streamlined procedures and cost-saving measures, chances are it's not a clinic at all but an advertising law firm interested in cashing in on the vanguard of a popular trend. The reverse may also be true—not every clinic calls itself one. Look for the hallmarks to determine if you are in good hands.

THE OUT-OF-TOWNERS

Finally, a word about going out of the neighborhood for your legal assistance. From time to time one hears of a client who is convinced that there isn't a single lawyer within state boundaries capable of handling his affairs. Anxious to impress his peers or overwhelm his adversary, this client is apt to hire a famous attorney from out of town. The selection is usually based on the number of books the lawyer has authored or the number of his more colorful cases that have made the news or have been scripted for the movies.

The client is apparently of the view that the big name will cause everyone else to pack up their briefcases and go home. It has been my repeated observation, however, that hired guns from out of town rarely carry the day. To begin with, the laws are different from state to state and, at times, from town to town. The "foreigner" had best do his homework. In addition, the out-of-stater, unless licensed to practice in the client's state, has to apply for permission to handle the case.

There are more practical considerations, too, which put the out-of-towners at a distinct disadvantage. They do not know the neighborhood ropes and are not on a first-name basis with the bureaucrats and paper pushers. They have no friends in town to help smooth the way or get things done. And worse still, they are often resented by the locals.

In most instances, the out-of-towners accomplish only two things: they make your battle more difficult and more expensive. (Bear in mind that you pay transportation costs, long-distance phone bills, and expensive hotel suites that double as makeshift offices; you buy breakfast, lunch, and dinner as well as the underwear and socks your attorney forgot to pack.)

If you feel that your affairs are such that you really *must* have Mr. Mighty from Ivy League U—, your next best course of action is to couple his services with those of local counsel to give him a home base. In this circumstance, serious consideration should be given to whether you can afford two lawyers and whether the pair can work together as a team. Egos being as inflated as they are in this profession, it must be clear from the outset who is in charge of what and where the buck stops.

❖

CHAPTER THREE

Shop Around

IT IS A DULL and at times exasperating job to compile a list of candidates and arrange interviews with persons who are likely to fit the profile of an ideal lawyer you have developed. Carelessness or the impulse to go with the first recommendation you receive, however, is to do yourself a profound disservice. At last count, there were in excess of 650,000 licensed attorneys in this country, and roughly 35,000 graduating from ABA-approved law schools each year. The American Bar Foundation reports that Washington, D.C., has the highest concentration of lawyers, with one per every sixty-five persons; New York has the lowest, averaging one lawyer for every four hundred persons. Fifteen percent of the lawyer population are women. Close to 70 percent of all lawyers are in private practice. With numbers like these, you can afford to be selective.

Just how much time and effort you should commit to locating prospective lawyers depends upon the nature of your problem, the amount of money at risk, the seriousness of the consequences, and the principle at stake. How important is it to you to get the job done right? If you are thinking of making a sizable investment in real estate, for example, or believe you have a terrific case of sex discrimination in the office, you would be foolish not to take the time to compile a list of worthy candidates for consideration. It's a question of whether you want actively to *choose* a lawyer or simply be satisfied with the luck of the draw. An efficient consumer will shop around and compare. Accordingly, set your sights on compiling a roster of three candidates for commonplace problems and double that if you have big problems, high stakes, or a lot of money to worry about.

FINDING YOUR CANDIDATES

There are numerous sources to tap in your effort to compile a solid list of potential attorneys, and you should canvass several. Just as a single recommendation could prove fatal, no one source should be favored over the others. Even the recommendation of a most valued advisor should be cross-checked with another source.

Friends: The most obvious and frequently consulted source for recommendations is your family and friends. Unfortunately, this can also be one of the least reliable resources available to you. A casual recommendation, proferred in the spirit of trying to be helpful, tells you little more than an arbitrary selection of a name out of a phone book. If you plan on turning to family or friends, be certain you establish the basis for the recommendation. Has the family member had personal experience with the recommended lawyer, or is he simply a next-door neighbor, golfing buddy, or someone a cousin twice removed used a few years ago? If personal experience was involved, was it with respect to a matter similar to yours? Was the client satisfied? How could the service have been improved? Would he or she call the lawyer again?

You should also inquire whether the person making the recommendation will receive any benefit from passing the name along to you. Will the recommended lawyer be sending along a gift as a token of his appreciation? Or perhaps the benefit is more subtle. It may be, for example, that the friend making the recommendation is a client of that lawyer and expects better service as a result of the recommendation. This can cut two ways. If your friend is a *valued* client, the recommendation could serve you well. No lawyer wants to disappoint his or her important clients and would not jeopardize the relationship by performing in a shoddy or careless manner where you are concerned. On the other hand, if your friend's case is not one of the lawyer's rain-making accounts, your friend may have reason to expect better service as a result of the recommendation, but you certainly do not.

If the friend or relative is tied to the legal community in some way, his or her thoughts on whom to interview are more valuable. This is particularly true if your problem falls within the expertise of the person making the recommendation. Lawyers tend to know lawyers in the same or related fields but would be hard pressed to come up with a name in an unrelated area of specialization. Now why, you might be wondering, would you ask your uncle the divorce lawyer for the name of someone to handle your divorce? The answer is simple: You should never hire a close friend or relative to act as your attorney. To do so handicaps your ability to complain, demand, and if necessary, discharge the lawyer. The first thing students learn in law school is to avoid the family and the affairs of friends—it's too messy, too much is expected, too little is paid, and an unfavorable outcome can cause a rift that could be perpetuated for generations. Rather than be offended, your uncle should be relieved that you are only coming to him for a recommendation and not as a client.

Other professionals: Other professionals with whom you deal may also be a valuable source for recommendations. A real estate agent, for example, could probably recommend a lawyer to handle the purchase or sale of your home or other property. An insurance agent or physician is no doubt able to refer you to a lawyer who handles personal injury claims, negligence actions, or products liability cases. The neighborhood church, single parent's group, or family counseling center might well be able to recommend an attorney who handles divorce, separation, adoption, and other domestic relations problems. Similarly, a trusted bank officer, your accountant, a securities analyst, or a stockbroker is in a position to recommend a tax, business, or estate planning lawyer.

Each of these recommendations, like those of your family and friends, deserves to be explored carefully. Does the person making the recommendation have a good and specific reason for believing that the attorney is really all that he or she is reputed to be? Is there any self-interest involved?

You should also bear in mind that professionals tend to associate along the same or similar lines of ability. While this is hardly a universal law, the chances are that if you are happy with your nonlegal professional, you should take the time to interview the lawyer he or she recommends.

Members of the legal community: Apart from lawyers whom you know well enough to call upon for recommendations, there are two other sources among persons affiliated with the legal community whom you should consider phoning. The first and often extremely helpful source is law school professors. In most instances, professors are well situated to give an unbiased assessment of the available talent in your community, and they are usually delighted to share their thoughts on the subject. Teaching affords them the opportunity to be well acquainted with who is doing what in their field, who has a good reputation, and who should be avoided. Moreover, some law school professors also teach continuing legal education to practicing lawyers, which gives them a good indication of which lawyers are interested in sharpening their skills. A phone call to the dean's office or the office of administration can provide you with the name of the faculty member who teaches in the area of your interest.

Persons who work in the court system on a daily or regular basis such as stenographers, court clerks, secretaries, or bailiffs constitute a second source of information. These people are well positioned to observe the best and the worst of lawyering. Their opinion is worth an inquiry particularly if you are in the market for a litigator.

Advertisements: As was noted in Chapter 2, thanks to a Supreme Court ruling in 1977, lawyers are now permitted to advertise. Prior to this opinion, lawyers were barred from advertising ostensibly to protect the unwary from deceptive, manipulative, and exaggerated claims. It was also the general opinion of the bar at large that advertising was unbecoming to a profession that was supposed to be more interested in serving mankind than in generating business.

The laws governing lawyer advertising vary from state to state. As a general proposition, however, lawyers are permitted to advertise their name, address, phone number, availability, and areas of practice. Advertising that is false, deceptive, or misleading is still prohibited, as are claims as to the quality of the service offered. The latter includes subjective, laudatory statements because they are not susceptible to measurement or verification. As such, promotional statements such as

"We're Number One," "Superior Service," or "The Best Divorce in Town" are prohibited in most places as being inherently misleading.

As with any ad, you need to be suspicious of what is for sale. If the law firm has used an advertising agency, a press agent, or a marketing group, the result will probably be an eye-catcher. Look for the fine print, and be certain to check the person out with another source before you conclude that he or she merits an interview.

The American Bar Association recommends that if you like the ad, ask the attorney for client references before you take the time to interview the person. While you won't always receive the references, there is no harm done in asking. The ABA also recommends that you keep a copy of the ad (or notes if it is a broadcast) in the event that you need to make a claim in the future about overreaching or the failure to deliver what was promised.

Directories: There are a number of directories available that list names and addresses of lawyers. Among the most popular of these, and generally regarded as the most comprehensive, is the *Martindale-Hubbell Law Directory.* It is arranged alphabetically first by geographic location and then by the name of the lawyer or the firm name. It also includes the attorney's address, age, phone number, law school credits, professional associations and activities, fields of practice, writings, honors, and at times, clients. In addition to this thumbnail biography, *Martindale-Hubbell* includes a rating system on the basis of confidential information solicited from other lawyers. An *a* rating indicates the highest level of competence, a *b* is high to very high, and a *c* is from fair to high. Apart from competence, an effort is also made to quantify integrity. A *v* rating indicates a very high character and a person who "embraces faithful adherence to ethical standards, professional reliability and diligence." It is the only measure of integrity offered.

While the biographical portion of the *Martindale-Hubbell Law Directory* is very useful to you in terms of learning an attorney's track record, not much weight should be accorded to the rating system. By providing anonymity to the peer group making the evaluations, some critics have suggested that ratings are passed out for reasons other than competence and integrity. Indeed, a high rating may at times reveal nothing more than how adept the lawyer is at socializing, rather than his capabilities as an attorney. What's more, a lawyer has to be in practice for at least ten years in order to be eligible to be rated at the highest level, and once it is obtained, there is a reluctance to reevaluate. The rating system also favors larger firms and excludes law partnerships and professional corporations. As such, many fine young attorneys and those associated with smaller firms or in practice for themselves may go unnoticed.

As the *Martindale-Hubbell Law Directory* consists of seven very large volumes, it is not the kind of thing you should plan on buying. Most libraries have a set in the public reference room, however, as do most law firms, law schools, and county and municipal offices. On the whole, it is easy to locate and well worth your time to do so.

A second helpful directory is *The Lawyer to Lawyer Consultation Panel Directory,* available only to the legal profession, and commonly referred to as a listing of lawyers' lawyers. The consultation panel is a national group of attorneys who have been selected on the basis of their expertise and leadership in their field to give advice to other lawyers as it pertains to their field of concentration. The lawyers who are invited to serve in this capacity have distinguished themselves on the basis of the number of years of practice in a given field, their participation in advanced education and academics, authorship, bar leadership, experience in government, and other notable accomplishments. If you know of a lawyer who has a copy of this directory, it can be valuable to you in your search for promising candidates.

Another useful directory and often available in libraries is the *Lawyer's Register by Specialities and Fields of Law.* This is a national directory that is distinguished for its categorization by specialization. It too lists some biographical data and also includes a fairly sizable listing of the names of attorneys who work for corporations.

In addition to these three directories, a number of other law lists are available, including state and regional compilations, directories of attorneys who specialize in banking, commercial, and negligence fields, and international law listings. If these are of interest to you, check your library, county clerk's office, or other public information source in your area.

Student legal services: If you are a student in search of a lawyer, do not overlook the possibility that the college or university with which you are associated provides legal counseling or a referral service. Student legal services have increased in popularity over the last ten years. Most of these services are funded from student fees and are quite inexpensive. Stan Pollack, seasoned staff attorney at the University of Michigan's Student Legal Services Office, estimates that "roughly three thousand students a year obtain legal services, each for about the price of a pizza." Some programs, such as the one provided by the University of Maine, Orono campus, even give students the opportunity to work on their own cases. This is not only a tremendous opportunity to see what lawyering is all about but a boost in one's confidence that the matter is under control.

Company and union representatives: If you are affiliated with a company or a union, find out if there is an attorney on staff. If so, this person is a good resource for recommendations, provided that he or she is able to exercise free choice and is not constrained by the organization's policy.

As always, be certain to ask if the company or union representative has had any personal experience with the attorney he is recommending. Has he sent others to this attorney, and did their problems resemble yours? Can you expect to be charged a consultation fee? Will the company receive any benefit from making the recommendation?

Legal referral services: Another source for recommendations, which has been around since 1937 but which has gained popularity only in recent years, are the so-called lawyer referral services. Designed to put citizens in touch with lawyers, these programs are operated by state and local bar associations and are located in over three hundred cities.

While the administration of such programs varies widely, the basic idea is as follows. A person in need of a lawyer phones his local bar association, who puts him in communication with the referral office. Some referral offices assign an attorney over the phone on the basis of geographic location alone without making an effort to determine one's needs. The better services, however, such as the programs operated in St. Louis and Philadelphia, schedule an appointment with a staff attorney on the referral panel. This initial consultation is either free of charge or will cost up to twenty-five dollars and runs about a half hour. Oftentimes, the problem can be solved during the initial consultation. If more help is needed, however, the person is given the name of an attorney. It is then up to the client to arrange a meeting where an appropriate course of action and fee schedule will be discussed.

While the system sounds good, a closer look at how it operates can help you decide whether the program in your area is worth your time and effort. To begin with, find out who operates the service and how they are funded. Adequate staffing and a sizable budget are essential if the service is to be effective. You should also inquire how lawyers are selected for the program. You may learn that any licensed attorney can put his name on the list. As such, you may ask yourself why any competent attorney with a booming practice has time on his hands. Likewise, if attorneys have to pay a fee to join or to obtain a referral, this is a sign that the attorney may be unable to attract clients through conventional means. You should also ascertain whether attorneys who have been the subject of disciplinary proceedings are barred from participating. And while we're on the subject, find out if participating lawyers are required to carry malpractice insurance.

In investigating a referral service, another important area of inquiry is whether an effort will be made to match you up with someone who is located in your area and who is capable of handling your type of problem. Some referral services operate on a rotation basis; the next case is assigned to the next name on the list whether or not that person knows anything about the area of law at issue.

Before you meet with the attorney you are assigned, you should determine how much information you can expect to receive. Will you, for example, be expected to pay that person another consultation fee? Is that attorney free to decline your case once he hears the specifics? If not, you are running the serious risk that he or she may be either uninterested in you or unequipped to deal with your problem but stuck with your case nonetheless. You might also ask yourself why any good attorney would get himself in the position of not being able to refuse a case. Is he participating in the program to build up a practice or did he join pursuant to a commitment to do his part in improving the delivery of legal services in the community?

What if you run into problems with the attorney you were assigned? Are participating attorneys monitored or reviewed in any way? Are clients requested to evaluate the lawyer at the conclusion of the case? Does the referral program offer arbitration or mediation services in the event a dispute arises? If such services are available, are they staffed only by lawyers? If so, you can be sure that such a panel is not predisposed to be sympathetic to your side of the story.

Another important area of inquiry is the kind of cases they handle. As a general proposition, lawyer referral services concentrate on matters such as divorce, family counseling, adoption and other domestic relations problems, consumer protection, negligence, collections, legal or medical malpractice, real estate, the problems of the elderly, social security and pension matters, traffic offenses, workers' compensation and disability, tax problems, estates and trust work, immigration, and occasionally, minor criminal difficulties.

Despite the many causes for hesitation covered above, there are some fine services available, and by asking a lot of questions, it is possible to determine if your area offers one of the better programs. If you decide to go this route, call your local or state bar association for the number or check the yellow pages under "Lawyer Referral Services." You might also consider obtaining a copy of the ABA's *Lawyer Referral and Information Service Reference Handbook,* which is a detailed and comprehensive catalog of state and local referral organizations indexed according to the services each offers. The ABA also publishes a shorter directory of lawyer referral services, which simply lists names, addresses, and phone numbers.

Public Interest, Government Agencies, Legal Aid, and Public Defender Offices: If you find that you can't afford a lawyer, there are still a few alternatives available to you. (See also "Alternatives to Paying the High Cost of Legal Fees," in Chapter 4.) The first of these are public interest groups. If your problem or difficulty falls within the ambit of civil rights; environmental concerns; discrimination on the basis of age, sex, race, or religion; consumer fraud; or similar "public" issues, your best bet is to get in touch with a public interest group that handles those issues. Such groups include the American Civil Liberties Union, the National Association for the Advancement of Colored People, the Native American Rights Fund, Common Cause, the Lawyers Committee for Civil Rights under Law, Public Citizen Litigation Groups, and the National Organization for Women, to name a few. Your state or local bar association should be able to direct you to an organization that addresses your needs. The competence, effectiveness, and political inclinations of public interest organizations vary, so be cautious in your selection.

Apart from public interest organizations, you should give some consideration to finding the appropriate governmental agency that handles civil rights violations, labor relations, and environmental concerns. Agencies such as the Equal Employment Opportunity Commission, the National Labor Relations Board, and the Environmental Protection Agency wield great power, and if they take your case on, you can be confident that they will see the matter through to the end. Check the blue pages of your phone book or the white pages under the heading "United States Government." You could also seek assistance from your local bar association, which should be able to supply you with the name of the agency most likely to handle your needs.

A last alternative available to you is the Legal Aid Society and Public Defender offices. Funded by federal and/or state government, bar associations, public interest grants, and private contributions, their services are free to persons who qualify as "poor" under the definition of the Federal Legal Services Corporation or standards of the local funding organization. Though attorney's fees are waived, a client *is* expected to pay the costs associated with the case.

The truth about these services is that their staff attorneys are tireless, dedicated, and overworked, their resources are limited, and the caseload is overwhelming. Not only are they chronically underfunded, but the uncertainty of their financial condition is a perpetual problem. Staff attorneys, while extremely well-motivated, have a difficult time fighting off frustration and some become worn down by the relentless problems of the poor. Adding insult to injury, staff attorneys are often faced with the resentment of persons of moderate income who are offended by the notion that poor people are provided representation at the expense of the working class while their own financial constraints put legal services out of reach. All these problems undercut the effectiveness of Legal Services and Public Defender offices. Nonetheless, if you are in need of an attorney and cannot afford one, contact your local office to make an appointment.

NARROWING DOWN YOUR LIST

If you have taken advantage of the above resources, you have no doubt collected quite a few names of potential attorneys. To narrow your list to a manageable size—say from three to six attorneys—some further investigation is required. Thus, it is in your interest to ascertain the education and reputation of each of your candidates before you take the time to interview. What you learn in this regard will assist you in whittling down your list to include only the most promising candidates.

Education: The easiest and most convenient way to ascertain an attorney's educational path is to consult the *Mar-*

tindale-Hubbell Law Directory, discussed earlier. Though the biographical sketches are concise, just about everything you need to know will be listed. Oftentimes the portion on education will consist of simply a line or two which may prompt a layman into underestimating the training involved. Lest you jump to such a hasty conclusion, consider, for a moment, the educational requirements an attorney must complete before he or she can practice law.

At the outset, the prospective lawyer has to finish college and then gain entrance to a law school, preferably one that has been accredited by the American Bar Association. The next three years consist of a tremendous grind plowing through a difficult and unfamiliar curriculum. In addition to the basics, there are some fifty electives a student can choose to study. On top of rigorous classwork, the motivated take on extracurricular activities, the more ambitious among these being *Law Review* (a scholarly publication put out by a student editorial staff). Following graduation, the student prepares for a two- to three-day bar examination, which tests raw knowledge of the law. Thereafter, the applicant must satisfy the Character and Fitness Committee of the State Board of Bar Examiners of his or her basic moral fitness to practice law. (Here is where one's politically active collegiate days may come to haunt. What is moral to wide-eyed, eager, and strong-willed college students does not often match the morality of crusty old bar examiners, who have been bullied about and sobered in the real world. The difference in perspective is enough to keep some applicants from being licensed.) If all is satisfactory, the applicant takes an oath to uphold and support the state and federal constitutions and is admitted to the bar.

This is a lot of education. You want to be sure that the candidate under consideration came out of it on his feet. To begin with, you should establish where each candidate went to school and what other degrees each possesses. An undergraduate degree in engineering, for example, is helpful if you have a patent problem. Similarly, a business degree is useful in corporate law, a chemistry or biology degree is an advantage in environmental law, a medical degree is useful in personal injury work, and so forth.

Do not make the mistake of being snobbish when it comes to where your candidates went to school. Even the best schools have graduated shockingly inept lawyers. What's more, a graduate of a prestigious law school, now working in an impressive law firm, is not likely to be interested in the affairs of mere mortals. If your case has possibilities of ending up on the evening news, or will make new law, the Michigan, Harvard, or Stanford graduate would be salivating. If all you want is a simple, quiet divorce, however, the hometown graduate would probably serve you well.

Reputation: As noted above, the facts of an attorney's education are fairly easy to track down. It will be more difficult to ascertain his reputation. Perhaps the best way to undertake this mission is to ask around the neighborhood. The opinions of other lawyers and former clients of your candidates will be the most valuable to you. Keep in mind, though, that reputation means different things to different people. For purposes of our discussion here, I will define it as involving both connections and character. An attorney who has both is usually reputed to be good.

Success as a lawyer, like a lot of things in life, depends heavily on one's connections. It is not simply what you know, but also whom you know. An attorney who has been around and made a few friends has a much improved chance at getting things done quickly and properly.

The second component to a good reputation is character. Certainly, a lawyer who persistently and deliberately fails to devote enough time to his cases or habitually misrepresents important facts is to be avoided at all costs. There are more insidious forms of cheating, however, such as billing a client for a coffee break or a three-martini lunch, or for the work the lawyer supposedly accomplished after he tied one on. Or consider the attorney who books himself into the most expensive suite the hotel has to offer or pads his expense sheet on some convoluted justification that he would not have bought that little trinket to pacify his wife but for the fact that your case is causing all the overtime and out-of-town travel. Or how about the person who takes your case on when she knows that it is way beyond her expertise but she is too greedy or too proud to refer the matter to abler minds?

The measure of a person's character is slippery business. Trust your instincts and ask a lot of questions that address the attorney's standing in the community. Is he active in the local bar association? Has he held office? Does the attorney devote any time to *pro bono* work? Has he ever been sued for malpractice?

You should also phone your local bar association to determine if any disciplinary proceedings have been brought or are pending against any of the candidates you are considering. While some bar associations will not divulge this information, a growing number will be happy to give you any information that is a part of the attorney's permanent record and not confidential. In California, the state bar receives on average two hundred calls a day of this nature.

As you will learn in Chapter 10, it is not often that an attorney gets into serious, justifiable trouble with a former client or the bar. When it comes to discipline, the bar is most reluctant to slap the wrists of a fellow practitioner, and as for malpractice, the expense, time, and obstacles keep most unhappy clients from pursuing this route. Accordingly, if the candidate has battled on any of these fronts, my advice is to move on. With such a large pool of capable attorneys available, you would have to have a compelling justification to consider retaining a person who has had a history of trouble.

At times, your conversations around the neighborhood may reveal that one of your candidates is somewhat of a popular or public figure. As a general rule, the fact that a lawyer gets his name in the paper a lot should not sway you. There are thousands of lawyers who do quality work, quietly and efficiently. Indeed, a fair argument can be made that the attorney who has kept his client's affairs out of the press has done that person a service. Even in highly newsworthy cases, a lawyer has to be extremely cautious when dealing with the press lest he be accused of materially prejudicing the proceeding. Legal battles are supposed to be tried in the courts, not in the papers.

SCHEDULING THE INTERVIEWS

Now that you have narrowed down your list of candidates to a handful of promising prospects, the next step is to set up interviews with each of these lawyers. The first person to phone is the lawyer you believe you are *least* likely to hire based on the information you have collected thus far. By starting with the least likely candidate, you have an opportunity to make a few mistakes and build your confidence for when it counts.

It is important that you speak directly with the lawyer, not a secretary or receptionist. After you introduce yourself, describe your situation in brief and then move on to the points outlined below. Be prepared to take careful notes, which will be useful to you when it comes time to compare responses. If you are not already accustomed to taking copious notes when dealing with professionals, it's a good habit to get into. You should be taking notes at every meeting and during every call with your lawyer from here on in. These are your permanent records, which can and usually do prove to be invaluable in ways you can't even begin to predict at this juncture. Note taking serves other functions as well—it both rivets your attention and is a signal to persons you are dealing with that the subject matter of your conversation is important to you and you intend to hold that person accountable for his views.

After you have explained your situation in brief, be sure to explore the following four points:

Area of expertise: It is essential to determine if your case concerns the type of problem the attorney commonly handles. You don't want to be a test case for him nor do you want to pay an hourly rate while the attorney educates himself in a new field. If the attorney shows the slightest hesitation over the subject matter of your problem, you had best seek assistance elsewhere.

Availability: Most good attorneys are busy, but very few like to turn business down. Make a point of asking whether the attorney is in a position to take on a new case and, if so, find out when you can meet. If the attorney is not able to meet with you within the next two to three weeks, chances are he or she is too harried to take on a new case but hates to admit it. A lengthy delay between your call and the scheduled meeting is also an indication of how quickly your work could progress should you hire this person. If the matter is pressing, don't hesitate to inform the attorney that you are most anxious to move quickly on it and see what he can do for you.

Costs: There are two kinds of costs to be concerned about at this juncture: consultation charges and the attorney's standard fee arrangement in cases such as yours. With respect to consultation fees, you will note that many attorneys forgo a charge for exploratory conversations, largely to encourage the calls of prospective new clients. You should not be put off, however, by the fact that some attorneys charge a nominal sum (no more than twenty to twenty-five dollars) to cover the time involved. An attorney sells only two things—time and expertise. It's worth the small fee to determine if he's got the talent you require. Bear in mind, however, that despite the modest sum you may be asked to pay, the consultation will not include detailed legal advice. The purpose of the meeting is simply to determine if you need a lawyer, the strength of your case, whether the attorney can handle it, and whether you like each other. While you should be favorably impressed by the attorney's ability to assess your situation at this meeting, constructive efforts to solve your problem begin after you hire someone.

The second area of costs—namely, a rough approximation of his standard fee arrangement for cases such as yours—is more difficult for the attorney to answer. It's not worth your time to meet, however, if the attorney's services are priced out of your range. On routine, nicely contained, fairly uncomplicated transactions (such as writing a will for a modest estate, buying or selling residential property, filing for an uncontested divorce, drafting standard corporate documents, reviewing a contract, and other commonplace problems), the attorney should not hesitate to give you a ballpark figure. His quote will be an estimate and will not include out-of-pocket expenses.

If your problem involves litigation, sensitive dealings, strong opposition, or any other foreboding complication, it is much more difficult for the attorney to quote you a range of costs. Be sensitive to the fact that difficult situations do not lend themselves to instant quantification. Nonetheless, press delicately for some idea of what you'd be saddled with ($1000? $5000? $10,000?). The following chapter discusses the question of cost at length. It's premature at this juncture, however, to establish more than whether a meeting would be a waste of time for both of you.

Business practices: Make a point of asking the attorney if it is his practice to confirm in writing the terms of any arrangements you reach. Though hard to believe, this question is more problematic for the attorney than the one about money. Lawyer-client contracts are still not common practice in the industry although clients are increasingly insistent on having one (see Chapter 6). Attorneys bristle with a natural reluctance to pin themselves down in this way. The fact is, however, that without a letter agreement covering the essential terms of employment and fee structure, the client has nothing more to fall back on, in the event of a dispute, than a general, oral statement concerning the services promised and the rate quoted. If the attorney is unwilling to confirm the bare bones of your agreement in a letter of understanding, it is prudent to seek assistance elsewhere.

PREPARING FOR THE INTERVIEW

Once your appointments have been scheduled, your next efforts should be directed toward preparing for the interviews. Preparation will save you time and calm your nerves. It will also assure that you get the most that is humanly possible out of your meetings.

Central to adequate preparation is a clear and concise statement of your problem, situation, or need. Give a lot of careful thought to identifying the circumstances that cause you to be in need of an attorney and take the time to write down the chronology of events or considerations that give rise to your problem. Include the names, addresses, and phone numbers of persons who touch upon your situation in either a material or a peripheral way. Jog your memory for dates of important meetings and central events. Your statement should include your time constraints—how quickly do you want this resolved? You should also mention not just your desired outcome, but the compromises you are willing to accept if things don't go your way. The statement should be brief (a page or two), but it should be precise and thorough.

In addition to a written statement outlining your problem or need as you define it, take some time to gather all important papers that concern your situation. Such documents may include, for example, correspondence, receipts, contracts, bills, estimates, agreements, deeds, insurance papers, canceled checks, photographs, and ticket stubs. If you aren't sure of the relevance of any particular item, include it and let your attorney be the judge. Make copies of these materials including the backs of checks or other documents that bear writing. The attorney you eventually hire will want to work with the originals, but during the interview phase of your search, copies are good enough. While you are at it, make a set of copies for yourself. Not only will it enable you to converse over the phone once you hire a lawyer, but things do get lost, misplaced, left in taxis, or thrown out by mistake.

The last step in your preparation is to compile a list of questions you want to be sure to cover during the interview. Chapter 5 will assist you in this regard. As you will note, such questions should not be designed to elicit legal advice but rather to determine if this is the person you want to hire. Once that decision is made, the legal advice will follow.

CHAPTER FOUR

❖

Understanding Costs

❖

PERHAPS THE most difficult aspect of an attorney-client relationship is that of cost. There are $40 billion in legal fees paid annually to private law firms in this country—and a lot of unhappy consumers to show for it. Law services do not come cheaply, but if you know what you are doing, it is possible to find or negotiate a fair deal.

As will be discussed in Chapter 5, cost is an important subject to discuss with each of your candidates during the interview stage. Depending upon the nature and complexity of your case, this part of your conversation can get very tricky. It is important to take the time to understand the details. This chapter will not only explain the available alternatives but also suggest ways to negotiate a more palatable fee than the one that may be quoted to you by any of your candidates. Though you may decide to negotiate with some of your candidates, however, you should not, as a result, feel obligated to rush into hiring an attorney who is amenable to your terms. No such obligation exists. Cost is but one part of the puzzle. Your objective is to develop a complete profile of each of your candidates before you make a hiring decision.

FACTORS DETERMINING FEES

Price is an important consideration in any decision to retain an attorney, but it is not the only consideration, or, indeed, the most important point where liberty or high stakes are at risk. In a complicated, pressured situation, the most expensive decision you can make may be to hire the cheapest lawyer on the block.

An understanding of what you are buying will save you time, money, and aggravation. Here are ten factors that play a role in setting fees. Their relative importance varies depending upon the individual attorney involved.

1. The nature of the desired service dictates in large measure the costs involved. The more routine and uncomplicated the service, the less time, labor, and skill is required, which should reduce the fee. Complicated matters demand research, strategy, consultation, extra staffing, travel, and possibly, court appearances. Similarly, if your matter concerns large sums of money, the extra effort and diligence involved usually commands a higher fee. The old adage "Time is money" is never more fully appreciated than here.

2. The attorney's reputation also enters into the cost equation. Superstars with a high success rate are expensive. So are specialists and attorneys who spend a large part of their day politicking and building ties with the forces that move the community. If you need this

kind of expertise and/or social clout, be prepared to pay for it.

3. The novelty and difficulty of your issues likewise come into play. A path-breaking case (such as paternity leave or the right of a homosexual couple to marry or adopt a child) costs you more. The attorney you hire not only must absorb every aspect of the existing state of the law but then must either shape your case to come within the legal limitations or devise a strategy to expand the boundaries in a society not predisposed to go your way.

4. The work load of the lawyer is a factor often overlooked by the client. If the acceptance of your case represents a lengthy engagement and/or the monopolization of existing staff, the lawyer is precluded from accepting other employment that might come his way. If you want to see a lawyer cry, catch him in his private moments after he has been forced to turn down a new and desirable matter because he's wrapped up in yours. Higher fees lessen the financial and emotional blow.

5. A prior relationship with the attorney also figures into setting fees. Repeat business or the promise of repeat business cuts your costs. On the other hand, if in past dealings you have proven yourself to be an irritating client, the chances are good that you will be charged a somewhat higher fee to make up for the aggravation.

6. The lawyer's assessment of the merits of the case is yet another factor that affects fees. As noted below, the lawyer has a variety of fee structures available to

him. Whether the fee is fixed or contingent will affect your costs. His choice in this regard depends in part on his analysis of the strengths and weaknesses of your matter. For example, if your case is one involving personal injury but your evidence is weak and your opposition strong, no lawyer (unless he's very hungry or unusually sympathetic) will take the case on contingency. Conversely, if your evidence is terrific and your opponent doesn't have a prayer, a lawyer's inclination would be to take the case on a contingency basis rather than on an hourly rate.

7. Minimum fee structures have been abolished—advisory fee schedules are still in effect in a lot of jurisdictions. As such, the going rate in the locality for the same or similar services is still a factor in an attorney's assessment of costs. This is less offensive than you might think—it takes experience to estimate costs properly. Unless the attorney has done a number of cases quite similar to the one you present, it makes sense that he'd check what his colleagues charge for the service you request. Without this information as a benchmark, his estimate might be too high or too low—*both* circumstances work to your disadvantage. The disadvantage of a fee that is too high is obvious. If a fee is too low, however, you run the risk that the attorney will lose interest in your case, hurry it along, or close it out in a quick and sloppy way.

8. The more pressing your matter, either due to your own desires or the demands of the circumstances, the more expensive. Expedited service commands a premium. Associates burn the midnight oil, social engagements are canceled, family and household responsibilities get put on the back burner, support staff get paid over-

time, and messengers are used to speed delivery. If you have to have it yesterday, be prepared to pay for it.

9. The client's ability to pay is a factor that comes into play at times. What hard heart would charge a little old lady an arm and a leg to keep her landlord from harassing her? If the chemistry is right, the cause pressing, or your attorney has been waiting for just such a case to cross his desk, a dollars-and-cents mentality may give way to nobler impulses.
10. Finally, overhead is a very large factor in setting fees. Impressive firms generate impressive fees. They have to—someone has to pay for the window dressing, the cavernous library, and subsidized associate lunches. Even with modest surroundings, however, it's expensive to run a law office. Studies show that 40 percent or more of a fee goes to overhead. Keep it in mind if you are served coffee in fine china when a paper cup would have done nicely.

FEE STRUCTURES

An attorney has a wide range of possibilities when it comes to structuring a fee. While the more common alternatives are set forth below, keep in mind that it's possible to fashion some combination of the available fee structures where the situation demands a hybrid approach and where the attorney is willing to be flexible.

Flat fees: A flat fee is a stated dollar amount for the service you require. As a general proposition, flat fees are offered in only the most routine matters such as for the preparation of a simple will, trust documents, articles of incorporation, simple contracts or partnership papers, name change documents, and papers for an uncontested divorce. Such matters are predictable, concise, no surprises, no alarms—just fill in the blanks and file it in the right place.

In most circumstances the flat fee represents a real savings. The exception is when a routine case turns out to be not so simple after all. An attorney in this position must either renegotiate the fee or speed the work along to cut his losses.

Hourly fees: When an attorney is not sure how much time it will take to complete a matter, he may propose that the fee be computed on an hourly basis. Hourly rates vary in accordance with the ten considerations discussed in the preceding section. In addition, the rates of the various stratifications of attorneys within a single firm vary. Seasoned senior partners may charge anywhere from $60 to $200-plus an hour. (Indeed, I recently heard of a New York City specialist's fee set at an extraordinary $350 an hour.) Junior partners and associates are considerably less. Paralegals run from $20 to $40 an hour. A cheaper hourly rate may not be a savings, however, if the person is less experienced and takes twice as long as he should take to accomplish his task. (For an explanation of the structure of a law firm, see "Assignment of Work" in Chapter 5.)

An attorney who bills on an hourly basis has to have some method of keeping track of his day. Most attorneys rely on time sheets where they record the amount of time spent for each client, each day. Here is where things can get sloppy.

Some attorneys are not vigilant about keeping track of the clock and will estimate their time expenditures at the end of the day (or, heaven forbid, the end of the week). Nobody's memory is that good. On a busy day, an attorney could perform work on half a dozen matters. Can he really recall with accuracy how many phone calls he placed and received, or how long he spent in meetings, researching, proofreading, thinking, soliciting opinions, daydreaming, and spinning wheels?

There are also the pressures of the boss to consider. In most firms there is an express or unstated understanding that associates must bill a certain number of hours a month to earn their keep. (In large firms, a computer printout arrives each month to inform the associate exactly how long he or she worked and how it compared to last month.) For the insecure or overly ambitious associate, the incentive is to pad time sheets: round up whenever possible; bill every phone call, however brief, at one-quarter of an hour; or overestimate library time because everyone knows research is like a black hole when it comes to time input. Where it could take one person an hour to comprehend a particular problem, another may spend eight hours, and there really isn't any way to judge whether all that time was necessary. The person who took one hour could have been luckier, smarter, or sloppier than his colleague.

One should also consider the business lunch. Whether it is a relaxed two-martini, *foie gras de canard* affair or a quick burger at the local diner, if business was discussed, the time (all of it) goes on your bill (so may the cost of the food, by the way).

The problems with the hourly rate are manifest. Unlike the flat fee, it is impossible to predict how much you will owe because you often have no idea how long the matter will run. The smallest complication can cause your costs to soar. In addition, an incompetent attorney or a slow worker can really drain your bank account.

There is a professed bright side to the hourly rate, however, and that is that you only pay for work that is actually performed. That's the idea, anyway. Since there can be a wide divergence between theory and practice, however, pay close attention to the bills when the meter's running (see Chapter 7).

Retainers: The term "retainer" has two distinct meanings in the law. First, when a client turns a sum of money over to a lawyer who has been hired on an hourly basis, the up-front money is called a retainer and is meant to cover the start-up costs of the case as well as the initial hours of work. In this sense, the retainer acts as an advance against fees and is commonly used in litigation or situations where the attorney is just beginning in practice and needs a little capital to get the case started. This is perfectly understandable and acceptable. You should be certain to state in the attorney-client agreement, however, that any unused portion of this retainer will be refunded at the conclusion of the case (see Chapter 6).

The other kind of retainer is a fixed sum of money a client pays on a regular basis, be it monthly or quarterly, in exchange for which he is guaranteed ongoing performance of routine services. Such a retainer is often used by corporations, for example, to lock in the ability to call for advice at any time on an as-needed basis. If this is the kind of retainer that interests you, it is imperative that you clearly specify in the fee agreement exactly which services are covered and which are not (see Chapter 6). Typically, the review of contracts, the rendering of an advisory opinion on a particular problem, and basic financial assistance are included in a fee structure of this kind. Litigation and complicated negotiations, however, are commonly presumed to be extra unless otherwise stated.

Where the amount is large or the money is to be held for a significant period of time, you should be certain to instruct the firm to invest your retainer in an interest-bearing account. The interest accrues to you.

Finally, you should only negotiate for a three-month or six-month time span, which will give you some flexibility to see if the arrangement suits your purposes. If it turns out that the fee is unreasonable in relation to the services rendered, you will need to rethink the arrangement to provide a more acceptable balance.

Contingency fees: Contingency fees are just what the name implies—fees that are *contingent* upon the happening of a specified event, usually the recovery of money or the successful resolution of a negotiation, the outcome of which is measurable in dollars. Both the client and the attorney share in the risk of an uncertain outcome; neither can be certain of the extent of their gamble. The client benefits by getting "free" legal services in exchange for which he or she agrees to pay the attorney a sizable percentage of whatever recovery the attorney wins. The attorney benefits because he can demand a higher percentage of the recovery, justified by the risk he assumed of no recovery. If the case is won, both are happy. If it is lost, the client is not obligated to pay anything in the way of fees. The out-of-pocket costs of the case, however, are advanced by the client in either event. If the attorney is successful, the costs will be reimbursed to the client and, in most cases, before the attorney's fee is calculated.

Contingency fees have been in use only about thirty-five years and are limited to cases where a money judgment is sought. Such cases include, by way of illustration, wrongful death claims, defamation and other tort claims, collection matters, and personal injury cases. The use of contingency fees is specifically precluded in other types of cases such as criminal matters and, in most localities, domestic relations cases. The rationale for allowing them in some cases and not in others turns on public policy. With respect to domestic relations cases, for example, it is considered detrimental to the good of society to allow an attorney to tie his payment to the amount of alimony, support payments, or the value of the property settlement he secures. In order to be paid, the incentive is to perpetuate the disharmony in family relations rather than to attempt to restore the peace.

Contingency fees are likewise precluded in cases where the amount owed the attorney exceeds the maximum ceiling provided by law. Every state has set a limit on the percentage an attorney can collect with a contingency fee. To find out the limits in your area, call your local bar association. It is also worth noting that a court may decide to reduce an otherwise lawful contingency fee where the judge rules that the fee is unconscionably high (such as in a circumstance where an attorney does very little work but winds up with an awful lot of money).

Much has been written debating the pros and cons of contingency arrangements. The proponents argue that this fee structure allows the poor and middle class access to the law where they could not otherwise afford to retain counsel. Advocates also argue that with a stake in the outcome, the attorney has a vested interest that will strengthen his commitment and dedication to the task at hand.

These good arguments notwithstanding, the opponents raise some serious concerns. They argue that contingency fees hold an inherent conflict of interest: If a good but not great settlement offer comes along, the attorney is inclined to advise the client to accept it rather than risk an adverse outcome on trial. The attorney might also be inclined to strong-arm a settlement simply to avoid the massive amounts of work necessary to prepare a case for trial.

The opponents also argue that the large percentages the attorney can demand are disproportionate to the amount of work involved and often take on the appearance if not the reality of a windfall to the lawyer. (Some critics go so far as to say that an attorney will take on only a case he knows he can win and since 95 percent of all civil litigation of this kind is settled anyway, the attorney is really cheating the client out of proceeds that should rightfully accrue to him.) Another disadvantage cited is the fact that if the attorney misjudges the strength of the case, he may lose interest in trying to win it—after all, he isn't being paid by the hour and the chances are good that it's a loser.

My advice is to *avoid* a contingency arrangement if you can afford some other arrangement. In recognition of the risks to a client in such circumstances, the ABA's Model Code of Professional Responsibility (adopted in some form in every state) provides that lawyers should decline to proceed on a contingency basis if the client can afford a flat fee, an hourly rate, or a comparable arrangement. The code also specifies that a contingency arrangement is prohibited unless it will be beneficial to the client. The Model Rules of Professional Conduct (the successor to the model code and currently under consideration—see Chapter 8) pretty much eliminate this approach. The rule governing fees does state by way of commentary, however, that where there is doubt whether a contingency fee is consistent with the client's best interests, the lawyer should explore other alternatives. (The ABA is not alone in their hesitation to endorse contingency fees—these fees are illegal in Canada, India, England, and most other European countries.)

My recommendation notwithstanding, if you conclude that a contingency fee is the only or best alternative available to you, it is essential that you spend some time educating yourself in the nuances. Contingency fees can and often should be negotiated. The remainder of this section explains how you can strike the best deal.

At the outset, call the state bar association and find out if contingency fees are allowable in cases such as yours and if there is a maximum percentage an attorney can demand. Assuming a contingency fee is legal in your kind of case, you must then determine whether it is desirable. To make this decision, it is helpful to have a basis for comparison. As such, your next efforts should be to determine how much the case would cost you if it were to be handled on an hourly basis. Ask each of your candidates to estimate, hypothetically speaking, the number of hours it would take to complete your work if the case settled early or late in the game or resulted in trial. To encourage a candid response to these questions, it is probably a good idea to refrain from telling the attorney that you are considering a contingency fee. Unfortunately, some attorneys' eyes will light up with dollar signs at the prospect of taking a good case on contingency. Accordingly, the inclination of such people would be to exaggerate the time and work involved so as to leave you with the erroneous impression that you will come out ahead on a contingency basis.

Let us say then that you have an idea of how much your case would cost you if it were being handled on an hourly basis. The next step is to assess your chances for an early settlement. The idea here is that if your case is likely to "settle out" rather quickly, it may be less expensive for you to enter into an hourly fee structure rather than a contingency arrangement. There are many factors to consider, the first being the doggedness of your opponent. If he believes himself to be in the right and is determined to see the matter through to the bitter end, the chances for settlement are slight. On the other hand, it may be that his guilt is clear and you think he will wave the white flag once you serve him with notice of trial. It is also possible that your opponent will desire to settle the matter, deliberately but gingerly sidestepping the entire issue of liability. Where the chances for settlement are good, it behooves you to think twice before you enter a contingency arrangement—and if you still go this route, you should negotiate to pay your attorney a lower percentage of the recovery than the maximum allowable by law.

A second factor to consider is the strength of your own case. If, for example, you are one of a number of people who initiated the suit (plaintiffs) and someone else's attorney is heading up the case, why should you surrender a full one third of the recovery (or the maximum contingency percentage allowable in your area) to your attorney when he is responsible for very little work? Numerous plaintiffs have the advantage of the strength in numbers approach and stand a better chance of forcing a settlement. If your attorney intends simply to monitor the case, attend a few meetings, and make a couple of phone calls, you may conclude that an hourly fee will be less expensive.

Finally, you should consider what is at risk for you. Whether your claim involves $50,000 or $500,000, the strategy is the same, the work is the same, and the lawyer's time input is the same. Logic dictates that the greater the dollar amount involved, the less the contingency fee should be—otherwise, your attorney stands to gain a fortune rather arbitrarily.

As a result of all these variables, negotiating a contingency fee can get tricky. Bear in mind that while there is a ceiling imposed by law, there is no such thing as a standard cut or a going rate. Indeed, you should propose a multiple-tiered structure or a sliding scale based upon work actually performed. Such an arrangement might suggest, for example, that the attorney be paid 20 percent of the recovery (after the reimbursement of costs) if the case settles quickly and painlessly and 30 percent if it goes to trial. Alternatively, you could reach an arrangement where the attorney would receive 20 percent of the first $100,000 of recovery and 10 percent of every $100,000 above that. You might also ask each candidate to consider combining a flat fee or an hourly fee with a contingency arrangement.

Whatever arrangement you reach, it should take into account all the possible outcomes and variables including the amount of the expected recovery; whether a trial will be likely;

how hard the attorney need work; whether your opponent disputes liability; whether there are other plaintiffs; how much the attorney should receive if you need to change counsel before the case is concluded; whether the costs of the litigation will be deducted before or after the attorney claims his fee (assuming he prevails or the case has been settled); and what the attorney should earn if you decide to discontinue the case (thereby preventing the occurrence of the contingency that is supposed to trigger his fee). The understanding should be specific and carefully detailed in the attorney-client agreement (see Chapter 6).

If you are embarrassed or uncomfortable with this kind of negotiating, you should steer clear of a contingency arrangement. And if an attorney gives you a hard time about this kind of discussion, you could either continue your search for an attorney you are more comfortable with or remind him that contingency fees invite abuse. The idea is to structure an arrangement for compensation that reflects realistically both the work and the risks involved.

Percentage fees: Contingency fees and percentage fees both involve the calculation of a percentage and for this reason are often confused. In fact, they are quite different fee structures. As we discussed, a contingency fee is a percentage of the outcome in a case that has been either won or favorably settled. A percentage fee, on the other hand, may be set when a matter involves the management or disposition of a specific asset or group of assets with a quantifiable value; the attorney's fee is a percentage of that value. As such, percentage fees are not typical in adversarial cases and are not tied to the outcome of any such controversy.

The advantage of a percentage fee is that a client knows in advance precisely how much the legal work will cost him. The disadvantage is that the attorney is being compensated on a basis other than the amount of work involved. His percentage is secure irrespective of whether the case is extremely difficult or extraordinarily easy.

Percentage fees are favored, for example, when a lawyer is asked to probate an estate, act as counsel to an executor of a will, or act as a receiver in bankruptcy. Another frequent use of percentage arrangements in some parts of the country is with the sale of a home—the percentage fee is frequently fixed at 1 percent of the value of the home.

Certain percentage fees are flexible and therefore can be negotiated; others are predetermined by law. If you have doubts as to the accuracy of what an attorney is telling you in this regard, phone your local bar association and find out the limitations involved, if any.

FEE SPLITTING AND REFERRAL FEES

In the old days, it was not uncommon for a client to hire one attorney and then, to his surprise, have his case referred out to a second attorney in a different firm. The second attorney, grateful for the referral, would pay the first attorney a sizable "thank you" or would even go so far as to split his fee. Who is paying for all this? The client, of course.

Today, there are strict limitations on such arrangements. The Model Rules of Professional Conduct and Model Code of Professional Responsibility (see Chapter 8 for a discussion of the difference between the two) state that an attorney cannot split fees with a person outside the firm unless a number of conditions are met. First, the division of fees must be in proportion to the services performed by each lawyer. (Alternatively, and if the client agrees in writing, a fee may be split where each lawyer assumes joint responsibility for the representaticn.) It is unethical for an attorney to receive a fee for work he did not perform. Second, the client must be advised of the participation of other lawyers and have no objections. Finally, the total fee to be paid by the client must be reasonable. While the rules do not define reasonableness in this context, a client is probably saddled with an unreasonable fee where he or she pays substantially more for duplicate efforts than if a single attorney had handled the case. (See Chapter 7 for a discussion of excessive fees.)

Ideally, a client should make certain that the attorney he or she hires is the one who intends to do the work. Failing this, a client who finds that his case is to be referred out should question the first attorney as to the necessity of the referral and the fee arrangements reached between both counsel. The client should also seek an explanation of the proposed division of work and whether both attorneys assume joint responsibility for the case. Finally, the client should inquire into the basis for the selection of the second attorney—is he an expert in the field or a colleague to whom the first attorney owes a favor?

OUT-OF-POCKET COSTS

When it comes to assessing what you can and cannot afford for legal services, bear in mind that fees are only a part (albeit the largest part) of the dent in your finances. There are transaction costs that you are responsible for in addition to the fee. These so-called "out-of-pocket" costs vary depending upon the nature of the work involved.

Typical out-of-pocket costs include filing fees; subpoena fees; witness fees; messengers; reproduction, printing, and binding costs; postage; medical reports; travel expenses; computer time; and consultation fees with accountants or other experts such as investigators, statisticians, or pollsters. In an unusual case, a trial attorney may feel that it is necessary to hire a behavioral scientist or psychologist to assist him in the selection of a jury. (Juror psychology has become a separate discipline in recent years, and there are consulting firms available whose sole business is to assist litigators during jury selection.) Whatever your case demands, each of your candidates should be able to provide you with a range of the projected costs.

STRIKING THE BEST DEAL

The smart consumer, educated through comparison shopping and apprised of market conditions, will look for an opportunity to negotiate when it comes to cost. The bite of competition, the elimination of mandatory fee schedules, and the abundant supply of talent make it a buyer's market. Certainly some lawyers will always have more work to do than they can handle. The majority, however, could use more clients.

Despite the latitude afforded clients, however, a surprising number still exhibit a reluctance to bargain—based, probably, upon some misguided notion that questioning costs is disrespectful or inappropriate. True, a lawyer's office is not an Arabian bazaar; it is also true that the days of unquestioning deference are over.

I am not suggesting that you bargain for the sport of it, but if during the course of your interviews you have learned that a range of prices is available for the service you seek, it is common sense to question a quote that seems too high. But keep your objective in mind: You are not seeking the cheapest service, but the lowest cost for the highest competence. If it's not quality work, it's no bargain. Likewise, if you manage to persuade a lawyer to do the work for substantially less than he or she should have agreed to, you may have sullied the relationship and jeopardized your chances for competent representation. Almost everyone resents being taken advantage of, and lawyers are no exception.

So now that you are disposed to bargain, how do you do it? Once you have conducted enough interviews to get a sense of the market, the way to begin with a high-priced lawyer is by pointing out that you have spoken with a number of other attorneys in his area and you believe the price he is quoting you is quite a bit higher than that of his colleagues. Even if the lawyer succeeds in persuading you that his high price is justified (he's more intelligent, more experienced, more successful, or faster), the fact that you have raised the issue alerts him to the fact that you are an educated consumer.

Another tactic you might consider is to point out any special features of your case. If it is uncomplicated, make a point of mentioning the routine nature of the services you require. Offer to structure a two-tiered fee schedule to protect the attorney if your "routine" case turns out to be a real nightmare.

If your case has social, political, or humanitarian dimensions, make a point of sharing this information with your attorney. Your case just might pull at his heartstrings, appeal to the crusader in him, or represent the opportunity to earn a little goodwill in the neighborhood (translation: more clients). Lawyers are business people, but many will acknowledge the public servant aspect of their profession. Indeed, some firms require each attorney to dedicate a certain number of hours per year to *pro bono* activities. In New York City, for example, 5,000 of the city's 35,000 attorneys have agreed to provide thirty hours per year per attorney to public service work—this is the equivalent of an eighty-person law firm dedicated exclusively to public interests.

Another bargaining chip that may be available to you is the possibility of supplying the attorney with more business in the future. If you think this is likely, mention it. It doesn't necessarily have to be your business. If you are part of a large corporation, social group, or community council, you should mention this in passing and leave the attorney with the impression that if he does a good job, your friends and colleagues will hear about it.

As a final note to striking the best deal, bear in mind that you should absolutely never allow yourself to be bullied or pressured by a fast-talking attorney. If you come across someone who does business in this way, thank him for his time, walk out the door, and don't bother looking back. There are plenty of other lawyers around who will be willing to be more flexible and who will respect your circumstances.

ALTERNATIVES TO PAYING THE HIGH COST OF LEGAL FEES

Despite negotiation of the best deal possible, legal services are expensive, and you may still discover that paying full price is out of the question. There are some alternatives if you qualify. (See also "Public Interest, Government Agencies, Legal Aid, and Public Defender Offices" in Chapter 3.)

The first of these is prepaid legal expense insurance. It works pretty much the same way as medical insurance. In exchange for a premium, you are guaranteed a specified amount of legal coverage up to the maximum allowable under the policy. Like all insurance policies, inspect your coverage carefully as well as the claims process and the amount of flexibility you have in selecting your own attorney.

A second possibility, though uncommon, is that you might be able to recover legal fees from your opponent if you are successful in your action. While the general rule is that the prevailing side is not entitled to reimbursement from the loser, there are numerous exceptions carved out by federal statutes, and you should ask your attorney if any of these are available to you. (The most common statutes authorizing "fee-shifting," as it is called, are in the area of civil rights. These laws authorize the court to award reasonable attorney's fees to a plaintiff who has prevailed in a suit against the government.) Apart from these statutory exceptions, if you are a defendant and can demonstrate that the case against you was brought in bad faith, or was designed to harass you or cause embarrassment, you can instruct your attorney to make an application to the court for an award of costs.

A last alternative that may offer some relief from the high cost of legal care is prepaid legal service plans. The concept is simple: Specified legal services are available to plan members in exchange for the payment of membership dues. These plans, similar to insurance, work on the principle of spreading the risk among a large group of people with the assumption that only a small percentage of them will avail themselves of the benefits.

The first prepaid legal services plans came out of the efforts of policemen's benevolent associations and railroad brotherhoods in the 1930s to help members with employment problems get in touch with sympathetic lawyers. These plans were criticized and attacked for decades until a series of four Supreme Court cases culminating in 1971 put the matter to rest. In the same year, through grants by the American Bar Endowment, the American Bar Association, and the Ford Foundation, the Shreveport Bar Association established the first formally recognized prepaid legal services plan serving the Laborers International Union, AFL-CIO, Local 229.

Since this time, thousands of plans have blossomed. Alec M. Schwartz, Executive Director of the American Prepaid Legal Services Institute, estimates that "while ten years ago less than one million persons subscribed to some prepaid plan, today, the figure is closer to seven million." Schwartz projects that roughly twenty-five million people will be covered by group legal services plans by 1990 if the current tax laws remain in effect. (At present, Section 120 of the Internal Revenue Code allows employees to exclude from their taxable income both the contributions made by employers to group legal services plans as well as the value of any legal services they receive under the plans.)

Prepaid legal service plans are designed to accomplish three basic aims. The first is to improve the accessibility of legal services to persons of moderate income (50 percent to 70 percent of the population, depending on whose statistics you believe). The rich can buy Wall Street; the poor, with some maneuvering and persistence, may be lucky enough to avail themselves of the Legal Services or Legal Aid. But for the middle class, an unanticipated legal problem can be disastrous, to say nothing of the impossibility of their taking advantage of the counseling and future planning functions a lawyer can provide.

The second aim is to use the strength-in-numbers approach to secure the lowest cost for services. The bargaining strength of a group is formidable as compared to that of an individual. Not only are plan members assured of high quality at favorable rates, but the lawyer also benefits by being able to count on a certain amount of steady business from plan members and by being able to reduce the number of bad debts he usually suffers. The attorney has also gained by broadening his network of clients, which usually leads to more clients.

The third and final aim of such plans is to promote the concept of preventive law. In crisis situations, the most a lawyer can do is patch up the problem. With the advent of prepaid legal plans, however, participating members are more likely to get in touch with a lawyer before an emergency develops. Once membership dues are paid, the incentive is to seek help as soon as it appears necessary. Preventive law is the best service to obtain from an attorney. Not only can serious and isolated problems be averted but regular checkups can better address the overall legal needs of an individual or family.

Prepaid plans have been started by many bar associations,

private employers, schools, student groups, unions, insurance companies, and enterprising entrepreneurs. It seems that a plan is available for every conceivable combination of interests and needs. Some plans cover less than one hundred people; others have hundreds of thousands of members. Some use the services of a single attorney; others have hundreds on staff. Some cost as little as thirty dollars a year; others are considerably more. Some plans offer a toll-free phone number for unlimited consultation time; others provide for face-to-face meetings. Some plans require dues from members; in others, the employer or the sponsor foots the bill. There is also a wide range of coverage possible including non-work-related areas such as estate planning; divorce, separation, and other domestic relations problems; real estate; landlord/tenant; bankruptcy; personal injury; taxation; contracts; consumer problems; tort matters; traffic problems; minor criminal concerns; government benefits, and more.

There is such a tremendous variety in these plans, careful investigation is mandatory before you decide to join one. Find out who sponsors and administers the plan. How long has it been in operation? How many members does it have? Does the plan offer an open or a closed panel of lawyers or, possibly, a hybrid approach? (In an open panel, members are allowed to select their own lawyers; in a closed panel, the selection of a lawyer is limited to a roster of preselected attorneys.) How are the lawyers for the plan selected? How many lawyers are on call? What services are included and, importantly, what types of problems are not included? (The simpler the plan, the better. Some plans can get so intricate and involved that when you sort out all the ceilings, exclusions, and qualifications, you are hardly covered for anything of consequence.) How much are membership dues? Do the rates represent a substantial savings as compared to regular fees around town? Will the plan cover family members and other dependents? Does the plan offer any kind of grievance procedure if a dispute arises between a member and the lawyer?

If you need help in assessing a particular plan or in starting one of your own, contact The National Resource Center for Consumers of Legal Services (1302 Eighteenth Street, N.W., Washington, D.C. 20036; (202) 659-8514) or The American Prepaid Legal Services Institute, founded by the American Bar Association in 1975 (750 North Lake Shore Drive, Chicago, Illinois 60611; (312) 988-5752). Each organization acts as a clearinghouse for information and can provide sample plan documents, cost factor analyses, synopses of state and federal regulations, and other informative publications.

CHAPTER FIVE

Conducting the Interview

IN THE INTEREST of new business, most attorneys will be pleased to meet with you to discuss your problem but will do so only once. On the basis of this meeting you are expected to pick up enough information to decide whether or not you choose to hire the person. Careful preparation is essential. You'll have no problems in the interview phase of your search if you put aside any feelings of apprehension or intimidation and spend time deciding exactly what you want to accomplish before you walk in.

SUMMARIZE YOUR SITUATION

After the small talk about the weather or the trouble you had parking the car, you should be prepared to start the meeting off by identifying why you think you are in need of legal assistance. If you have done your homework as discussed in Chapter 3, it will be easy to articulate your problem or request in a straightforward, intelligible fashion without struggling for words, backtracking to include aspects you left out, or editorializing. Keep it simple, direct, and cogent—first meetings form lasting impressions.

The best place to begin is to remind the attorney of your previous phone conversation, which will help focus his or her attention on the proper subject matter. Then concentrate on identifying your interests, any competing interests, and the desired outcome. Don't divert the attorney's attention with superfluous matter. Once you have settled on whom to hire, there will be ample opportunity to fill in the details.

Special care should be taken to be as accurate as possible. This is particularly important if you anticipate litigation of any kind. It is a mistake to withhold pertinent facts, or worse, to shade or color the statements you do make. As you will learn in Chapter 8, a lawyer is bound to keep your secrets and confidences whether or not you decide to hire him. The purpose behind the rule is to encourage a free flow of information. Embarrassment or a guilty conscience on your part will severely hamper the attorney in his or her efforts to render assistance. So remember: A lawyer would much prefer to hear the bad news from you in the privacy of his or her office than from your opponent in open court or across a negotiating table.

YOUR EVALUATION

With the preliminaries out of the way, you should then concentrate on evaluating this candidate's qualifications. If you have done some advance preparation as advocated in Chapter 3 (see "Narrowing Down Your List"), you are already knowledgeable about the attorney's education and familiar with his or her reputation in the community. If a few questions linger with respect to these areas, however, the interview process is an opportunity to clear up any ambiguity.

In addition, and to assist you in covering all the relevant points to be discussed during the interview, the considerations that merit your attention are broken down into ten categories. They are:

Experience	Assignment of Work
Ability	Office Resources
Privacy	Conflicts of Interest
Communication	Expectations
Compatibility	Expenses

While some of your questions can be answered through observation alone, the majority will need to be articulated. Naturally, you should tailor your areas of questioning to suit each candidate. You will have to trust your common sense on which questions are appropriate, but at the same time, do not walk away unsatisfied on any important point. As a rule of practice, if you are not certain whether you should ask a particular question, ask it. If the answers you receive are hazy or confusing, quietly press for clarification. If still not satisfied, it is a safe conclusion that the attorney is either not concentrating or is hesitant to discuss the matter—neither is a good sign.

EXPERIENCE

An impressive education is something to take note of, but it is no substitute for experience. Excellent scholars do not necessarily make terrific lawyers. A classroom and a courtroom are very different settings. While law school lays the foundation, it does not teach the fine points of making an argument in open court before a hostile judge, the subtleties of addressing a jury, the mechanics of putting together and sweating out a corporate deal, the details involved in drafting a will, or the reporting requirements of government agencies.

Indeed, it has been argued in some quarters that the legal curriculum should be reshaped to resemble medical training, where a sizable portion of one's education consists of a closely supervised, "hands-on" training program. This would serve the dual purpose of instilling some practical knowledge and orienting a young lawyer's abilities. Some of the larger firms attempt to compensate for the absence of practical application by allowing first-year associates to rotate between each of the firm's major departments. The theory is that by sampling each of the disciplines, the new associate can make an informed choice about the career path he or she would like to pursue. In practice, however, the rotation system falls short of its purpose. In most cases, the time spent in each field is too short to be meaningful and too stressful to be contemplative. New at the job, the young associate is too busy trying to keep his or her head above water to test out the possibilities of the field.

The real legal education begins with work. Style, confidence, and substantive know-how are learned on the job. During the course of your interview, you should be sure to ascertain how long the attorney has been practicing and the type of work he or she concentrates on at the present time. You particularly want to know what percentage of the time he devotes to problems similar to yours and whether he is usually successful. If you expect your problem to involve trial work, for example, ask what percentage of the time the attorney is in court. If you need to close on a house, find out how many closings a month the firm handles. You want to be sure you know where your lawyer spends most of his energies before you conclude that he or she is suitable for you.

Apart from the practice of law, it is a good idea to inquire about other types of work experience, legal or otherwise, the attorney may have had. What you learn here may be of surprising advantage to you. With respect to other legal work, for example, an attorney who has spent time in the United States Attorney's Office will be a sure sight better trial lawyer than a person without comparable experience. An attorney who worked as an agent for the IRS before law school is likely to know his tax law. Work experience in nonlegal fields may be similarly productive. To provide but a few examples, a former real estate broker is no doubt versed in property law; a former union organizer is likely to know labor law; a former social worker is familiar with civil rights and possibly family law; and a former claims adjustor is knowledgeable about insurance law. Where possible, look for experience that represents the flip side of your situation. The best criminal lawyers are former prosecutors; the best pro-management labor lawyers are former union sympathizers; and so forth. Having worked for the opposition, the lawyer has the insight and confidence necessary to wage a vigorous battle. It is a tremendous edge if you can find it.

ABILITY

Ability is extremely difficult to gauge because it does not lend itself to quantitative measurement. While an attorney's success rate is some indication of competence, no two cases are ever alike and there is no guarantee that yours will be resolved to your satisfaction. Similarly, you should take only guarded comfort in the fact that the attorney has a good reputation. There is a tremendous difference between a soothing bedside manner and a solid command of the law.

Keep a sharp lookout during your interview for traits that might give you some clue as to competence. Consider the questions the attorney asks. Are they reasonable, pertinent inquiries? Is he or she methodical and concentrating? If your problem is complicated, is he taking notes? This is one way to assess whether he is serious about helping you.

Be wary of the attorney who purports to supply you with an on-the-spot answer or is confident of a speedy and resounding success. It is possible of course that your situation doesn't require legal assistance after all or that it involves a garden variety problem. Under these circumstances, it makes sense that the attorney is able to provide you with a solution without resorting to the library. More often, however, a ready-made answer is a sign of carelessness.

A competent attorney is one who can tell you if what you ask is possible, probably not possible, or out of the question. A thoughtful response is one that clearly identifies the nature of your problem, the practical considerations involved, and the steps the attorney plans on pursuing in order to resolve your situation. This kind of analysis shows a careful and reasoned mind.

Another indicator of ability is whether the attorney stays current in his or her field through continuing legal education courses and seminars. It's a terrific sign if the attorney teaches these courses from time to time—an indication that he or she is regarded as an expert in the field. The importance of advanced course work should not be underestimated. The law reflects and orders social relations—as these shift, reform, expand, and contract, so too does the law. Whole new legal disciplines may have blossomed and matured since your candidate was in school. The burgeoning interest in computer law and the rapidly unfolding area of children's rights are but two illustrations.

In thirteen states—Alabama, Colorado, Georgia, Idaho, Iowa, Minnesota, Montana, Nevada, North Dakota, South Carolina, Washington, Wisconsin, and Wyoming—continuing legal education is mandatory. Many other states are contemplating the enactment of advanced education requirements but the expense is a problem. William Wheeler, Executive Director of the Institute of Continuing Legal Education, affiliated with the American Bar Association's Division of Professional Education, states that "the flurry of activity a few years ago in this direction has really diminished. What the states are finding is that they can't afford to set up the bureaucracy to see such programs through." Even in states where continuing legal education is voluntary, however, the smart attorney carves time out of his schedule to sharpen skills and renew contacts.

Finally, a reliable, though often undervalued, indicator of competence is the degree to which the attorney enjoys his work. Everybody likes to make money, but the attorney who works only for the income and then does his best at the end of the day to forget about his cases is in my view destined to be less able than the lawyer who is stimulated by his work. The latter (no doubt an obsessive perfectionist) is more likely to double-check the fine points and put in that extra weekend. This is a person who strongly identifies with his work. Look for this attitude.

PRIVACY

Confidentiality and discretion are important components to a good working relationship. Although your attorney is bound by ethical considerations to keep your affairs private (see Chapter 8), you should be certain to stress the importance of confidentiality during your interviews. Avoid the attorney who appears prone to telling war stories about the humiliating details of your custody battle or the more sensitive aspects of your business transactions. While it is accepted practice among attorneys to compare notes about cases over lunch at the club, certainly no names should be mentioned. If the attorney you are interviewing strikes you as too much of a braggart, you might well expect to suffer some discomfort along these lines at some point in the relationship.

COMMUNICATION

One of the most critical traits an attorney can possess is his or her ability to communicate. If he can't get his thoughts across in a straightforward, intelligible, and engaging fashion, what good is he?

A good measurement of an attorney's ability to be precise and direct is the extent to which you understand him during the course of your interview. If his speech is littered with jargon or legalese, he has failed to make himself clear. And if you are having trouble discerning his drift, you can bet that your opponent, a judge, a jury, or your business colleagues will have the same trouble. A client should not have to decode anything his lawyer says or writes before it is comprehensible.

Another indication of a person's ability to communicate is his or her capacity to listen. A person who likes to prattle on usually hasn't stopped long enough to understand the issue or absorb your concerns. The inability to listen is deadly to effective communication.

Finally, the attorney's accessibility is a central component of communication. It doesn't do you a bit of good to hire an attorney who is simply not available to you. If he or she is overcommitted, you can expect that your calls will go unanswered for days. If you were kept waiting more than twenty minutes for your interview, or unduly interrupted by calls during your discussion, consider these indications that the attorney may not be available to you when you need him. Ask how far in advance appointments should be made. Find out his schedule, whether he is out of the office a lot, and the best time of day to reach him. The more time you expect your problems to consume, the more critical these considerations.

COMPATIBILITY

While it is true that you are seeking an attorney primarily for his or her knowledge of the law, bear in mind that the person you hire is also your representative and, in this regard, a reflection on you. As such, consideration should be given to whether he or she possesses the qualities of a person you want on your side. It boils down to this: Can you get along with the person? You don't need to be crazy about him or want to include him at every dinner party—you just have to have confidence that the two of you can work together for as long as it takes to get the job done right.

Sometimes, it's the little things that matter. Is he courteous? Does he attempt to put you at ease? Did he thank the secretary who brought in coffee? Can you tell anything about his personality from the books on the shelves, the magazines on the coffee table, or the art on the walls? Is he or she tied to the community? Do you like the looks of the place? If it matters to you, is he neat? (Due to my own disposition toward orderliness, I doubt I would feel confident with an attorney who had stacks of documents, a half-eaten yogurt and yesterday's newspaper strewn about.)

Is he warm, sympathetic, and gracious? While you should have no expectations of finding a surrogate mother or a psychiatrist, you are within your rights to expect a decent person who has the human capacity to care. A sympathetic ear, a warm heart, and feeling for a client's needs are basic to good lawyering.

Is the lawyer alert, energetic, and sharp? Is he interested in you? Interest and energy are mandatory given the difficulty and all too frequent tedium of the law. Some lawyers, for example, think nothing of keeping a client waiting despite an appointment fixed weeks in advance. I know of one attorney who would regularly excuse herself at the start of every meeting mumbling something about needing the comfort facilities. At first I chalked it up to coincidence. In time, however, I realized that this person was so habitually unprepared and overextended that she needed those extra fifteen to thirty minutes to sneak in a few phone calls to other clients or to collect her thoughts for the client she has kept waiting. These are not the actions of a professional who is energetic and interested in your cause.

Let me hasten to mention that the opposite extreme may also be problematic. It is possible for an attorney to be *too* interested in your case—so much so that it becomes his case and not yours. When ego gets in the way, you can no longer be sure that the attorney is making judgments in your best interests instead of his own. An attorney who advises against a good settlement offer, for example, motivated by a desire to take the case to trial and make a name for himself, has not done you any favors. An attorney who advises an appeal to the United States Supreme Court simply because of the prestige associated with arguing before that distinguished panel of jurists, and irrespective of the strength of your case, is acting frivolously on your time. An attorney who strong-arms your decisions, allows the case to gather its own momentum, or spends your money in ways calculated to garner publicity for the firm or to advance a personal crusade is a problem—your problem. Unfortunately, it is not always possible to detect this kind of overzealousness in your first meeting with an attorney. A sure clue to an eventual problem in this area, however, is that the attorney appears to possess an enormous ego.

ASSIGNMENT OF WORK

It comes as a surprise to the uninitiated that the person you are interviewing may not be the one who intends to do the work involved in your case. It happens with some frequency that there are certain partners in a firm who do nothing but *bring in* the business (that is, attend social gatherings, stay active in the bar association, shake hands, speak with prospective clients, crack jokes, make small talk around the courthouse, publish articles, and teach courses) and there are other partners who *keep* the business (i.e., do the work). Since these bait-and-switch tactics are common, it does you little good to be satisfied with the competence of the person you are interviewing if he or she is not the one who will be rolling up the sleeves and retiring to the library. Ask the person you are speaking with if he is the one who will be handling the case. If not, arrange to meet that person.

A word about the structure of law firms is in order. In all the larger firms and most of the smaller ones, there are various strata of lawyers. At the top of the heap are the all-powerful senior partners. These are the people who either formed the firm, inherited it, or dedicated such a large portion of their life to the office that they now own it.

Just under the senior partners are the junior partners. These are the lawyers who have been newly ushered into the fold and are still working hard to earn their new prestige.

Under the junior partners are the associates. Associates are junior staffers whose investment in the firm varies depending upon the length of time they have been employed. The more senior associates (averaging five to seven years of practice) are company men, nose to the grindstone, looking to make partner and find a more or less permanent roost. The more junior associates have much less of an investment in the firm. They are still forming judgments about the people they work with, the type of cases they are handling, their chances for longevity in the firm, and whether they should be revising their résumés and moving on.

In most circumstances, you should not be put off by the

fact that an associate will be handling all or part of your case. They are less expensive and often will devote more time and attention to your matter than would a partner. The reasons for this are twofold: First, associates tend to be unsure of themselves and often redouble their efforts as compensation for insecurity or a lack of experience; second, associates can count on their work being scrutinized by the partners, and it had better be good if they expect to move up the totem pole.

If your problem is particularly sophisticated, involves sensitive issues, or has political implications, you should insist upon a partner handling the matter. While an associate may possess an equal competence in the law, he or she may not have the political or social savvy necessary to resolve the case. Timing, tone, and instincts are acquired skills. At times, there is no substitute for experience.

While this hierarchy describes the vast majority of law firms in the United States, a new development is taking hold and deserves quick mention. In a notable departure from tradition, some firms have created a new job level opening as an alternative to the standard "up or out" policy. Coined "senior attorney status" by New York's respected firm of Davis, Polk & Wardwell, the first major firm to formalize this practice, the idea was to create a niche for senior associates who for one reason or another were not expected to make the grade of partnership. Often, the failure to make partner has to do with things other than competence, such as discrimination within the firm, a conflict of personalities, the associate's desire to start or raise a family, the inability to play golf, the associate's having too narrow a specialty, or the partners' reluctance to increase the size of the firm. The new category provides greater latitude in firm management. It allows the firm to mollify and promote talented associates who demand salary increases, without affording them a share in the management or ownership of the firm. This plan makes such good business sense, several firms, notably on the West Coast, have followed suit. In the event that you learn your case is to be handled by a "senior attorney," rest confident that he knows what he's doing.

OFFICE RESOURCES

Another component of your decision-making process is the quantity and quality of resources the firm has to offer. If your problem is relatively confined and straightforward, the question of resources should not be paramount. If you expect a lengthy involvement, however, or complications of any magnitude, it is helpful to ascertain how much staff and research-related support the firm can offer.

In addition, you should be interested in the resources of the firm if your problem involves an opponent and that person has significant resources at his disposal. In theory, the resources of your firm are not supposed to matter when it comes to sorting out the "justice" of your situation. Practice is another question entirely. At times, the disparity between the two firms tends to take on the appearance of King Kong versus Faye Wray. Regrettably, a mismatch in resources often proves decisive.

CONFLICTS OF INTEREST

Once you hire an attorney, you have a right to a full and undivided representation of your interests. Loyalty and dedication are presumed. If the attorney has an interest that conflicts with yours or affects his judgment when it comes to handling your work, his loyalty has been compromised.

A more complete discussion of conflicts, how they arise

and operate, is contained in Chapter 8. For now, however, make a note to include among your list of interview points a question about whether there is anything the attorney can think of which could raise a conflict of interest problem. While conflicts of interest are not always predictable, you are entitled to assurances right from the start that to the best of this attorney's present knowledge, no such problems exist.

EXPECTATIONS

In addition to sizing up each candidate, use the interview as an opportunity to voice your expectations. The sooner you articulate and agree upon your thoughts as to how the work will be conducted, the better care you are likely to receive. You should make a point of mentioning concerns such as how quickly you expect results, how frequently you require status reports, and how often you would like to converse.

Some clients are happy to turn the whole morass over to a professional and do not want to hear about it again until the work is completed. Others may feel that a great deal is at stake, and they are anxious to be apprised of all progress. Can you expect, for example, to receive copies of all correspondence and documents prepared on your behalf? Will you be notified of all significant developments? Will you have access to files maintained on your behalf?

Whatever your inclination, be candid about your demands. Your forthrightness will reduce frustration in the weeks to come and alert your attorney to the kind of communication that will make you happy. This foundation is important not simply to create a solid working relationship, but if problems do develop, you have an agreed-upon standard of performance to fall back on in stating your discontent.

EXPENSES

By no means should you conclude your interview without addressing the question of costs. If the attorney you are speaking with has not brought the subject up, do not hesitate to ask what the fee structure would be for the problem or matter you have outlined. As discussed in the preceding chapter, the lawyer should be able to give you at least a tentative idea of the financial basis upon which he or she would accept your case. If you cannot get him to identify the projected expenses, you should eliminate this candidate from your consideration. You do not need any surprises when it comes to money.

Now it may be that the price you are quoted sounds fair. So much the better. The opposite, however, may also be true. As you learned in the previous chapter, it is well within your rights to question a price that seems too high. If you have conducted enough interviews (or have otherwise acquired a working knowledge of the marketplace for legal services in your area), you should seize the moment and propose other possible ways of structuring the costs. On the other hand, if you are not yet familiar with the market, you might have to wait and rely on a follow-up call as an opportunity to bargain. In this circumstance, you could simply phone the attorney, telling him you were favorably impressed with his qualifications during the interview but were distressed over the price. With a compliment as your opener, you should then outline your proposal and mention any factors that may merit a fee reduction.

CONCLUDING THE INTERVIEW

Do not feel pressured to make a commitment at the conclusion of your interview as to whether or not you choose to hire this attorney. It is sufficient simply to indicate that while you are most appreciative of his time and consideration, you have others to speak with before you reach a decision and you will get back to him within a week or two.

CHAPTER SIX

The Formalities

IF CAREFUL INTERVIEWS were conducted, one should be able to eliminate at least half the candidates from the running. Presumably, any of the remaining lawyers would be perfectly capable of handling the job. How, then, to decide among them, formalize your relationship, and get things moving?

DECISION MAKING

Objective strengths and weaknesses notwithstanding, the decision on whom to hire should ultimately rest on a subjective analysis. Although you have carefully screened your candidates so that each of your finalists is technically competent, many legal problems require a level of trust that goes beyond professional expertise. You have to feel confident that the lawyer will not embarrass you or injure your interests. As such, most clients tend to select a lawyer with whom they have a lot in common to assure that they will be speaking the same language. If in the course of relations a friendship develops, consider this a bonus.

Once you have made your decision, common courtesy requires that you take the time to write a brief note of thanks to the lawyers not selected for the job. Each has parted with valuable time and is entitled to know where he or she stands. And if you are not persuaded by etiquette, consider the possibility of having to change or replace counsel midstream. One of the now-rejected candidates may be just the person necessary to fill a vacancy at a later date.

ATTORNEY-CLIENT AGREEMENT

The very first thing that should occur when an attorney is retained is that terms of the employment be formalized in a letter of understanding, or an attorney-client agreement. This is the best way to assure that there are no honest miscommunications and that each of you fully understands what is expected of the other. If you are not diligent about obtaining this agreement, you expose yourself to serious risks if problems develop in the months to come. Without a written agreement, a dispute about what is owed, what services were promised, or when the work was to have been completed becomes a swearing contest—your word versus the lawyer's. In the interest of harmonious relations, even the bar associations are beginning to advocate that one take the time to get all these points down on paper.

The attorney-client agreement need not and indeed should not be a lengthy document. The essential points are these:

Description of the service: A provision of the agreement should clearly set forth the services the firm has agreed to provide as well as the name of the attorney who will be responsible for the work. The description should be as specific as the circumstances will allow. In addition to describing the basic service, the agreement should refer to the attorney's obligation to answer the client's questions and explain the pertinent laws.

Fee: As you learned in Chapter 4, there are a variety of ways to handle the costs of the work you require. Once you and your attorney reach a decision about how to structure the fee, the fee arrangement as well as your agreement on how fees are to be computed should be specified in the attorney-client contract. For example, if you agreed to an hourly billing, you should request that the agreement specify not just the attorney's rate but the rates of other, less experienced persons who will be working on your case such as paralegals and associates. The rate at which support staff time is charged should be considerably less.

The attorney-client agreement should also provide an estimate of the total cost of fees assuming the attorney is able to make a reasonable judgment in this regard. Some cases, such as those involving litigation, simply do not lend themselves to reliable advance quantification. Dilatory tactics of your attorney or from your opposition, liberal discovery schedules (i.e., a set time period within which both parties are authorized to pursue the discovery of information pertinent to the case), tangential fights over confidentiality or other privileged matters, and a flurry of motion papers are among the countless factors that may render time and costs uncertain. The client must live with this. Other matters contain less uncertainty, and costs can be predicted with fair accuracy. Where a meaningful estimate of the total cost is not available, the client should request that the agreement specify a range of costs that takes into account the various contingencies that may or may not come to pass.

Ancillary costs: A lawyer's fee is only part of the total cost of the case. The client is also responsible for the payment of ancillary or so-called out-of-pocket costs. While these can rarely be predicted with accuracy, an estimate or range of possibilities should be stated.

Billing: A provision of the agreement should specify that monthly itemized bills are to be provided. An itemized bill is the most essential document you can have in terms of being able to monitor the progress of your work and the attorney's performance (see Chapter 7). This provision should also state the manner of payment that is acceptable to the lawyer.

Payment obligations: In most cases, a client is obligated to pay the bill within a short time of its receipt. If the attorney and the client have reached some other understanding with respect to when payment is owed, however, the terms of this agreement should be specified. For example, if the case is being handled on a contingency basis (see Chapter 4), the attorney-client agreement is likely to specify that the fee, if any, is not owed until the conclusion of the matter but that payment of ancillary costs is to be forwarded within seven days from receipt of the invoice.

This provision of the agreement should also specify the payment obligations of the client in the event that the attorney is discharged or forced to withdraw from the representation. (See Chapter 9.)

Timetable: Certain types of cases, such as the preparation of estates and trust documents, corporate papers, contracts, or deeds, lend themselves to prompt resolution. Other cases are too unpredictable to enable a lawyer to guess as to how long they might take. Where possible, an estimated timetable for the completion of services should be specified. In the event that it is not possible to predict how long a matter will drag on, and if the client is anxious for a speedy resolution, the agreement should at the least state the client's desire for a prompt conclusion.

Amount paid: If the client is obligated to advance a sum of money to the lawyer at the start of the case, the attorney-client agreement should specify the nature of the payment: Is it an advance payment against an unearned fee? Is it a retainer for services to be rendered pursuant to an ongoing relationship? Is it money to be held in escrow pending the settlement of litigation, for example, or the closing on a home? Is it money to be held for another or for payment of a fine?

The agreement should also specify the amount to be forwarded, how it is to be held, the bank account number, how it will be invested, and the frequency with which the client can expect statements as to the management of this sum. In no circumstance should an advance payment be deposited into a firm account. It is unethical for an attorney to commingle a client's funds with those of the firm or his own. Indeed, such an activity ranks among the top two most frequent forms of misconduct that give rise to disciplinary actions. (The other offense is neglect; see Chapter 10.)

Total cost: Finally, the agreement should specify the expected total cost or range of costs. If there has been any conversation about a bonus, the agreement should reflect the amount discussed and conditions for payment.

Although the attorney-client agreement is largely (but not exclusively) for the benefit of the client, it makes sense to have the lawyer draft it. There is an inherent conflict of interest in such an arrangement, but it is within the lawyer's capabilities and should be provided at no extra cost. Moreover, the client is protected with the ability to veto any provision he or she does not understand or like. The agreement should be reviewed, line by line, phrase by phrase, and anything that does not make sense should be questioned. Once the specifics have been ironed out, each party should sign and retain a copy in a safe place.

MODEL ATTORNEY-CLIENT AGREEMENT

If you are uncomfortable with having the lawyer preparing the agreement, take the initiative and prepare the contract yourself. Reprinted here is a sample attorney-client agreement that can be used as a model. Bear in mind, however, that state law may make some of these provisions invalid or undesirable. You may also want to include other provisions not here mentioned.

In the event that your case is being handled on a contingency basis, you might want to include some or all of the following contract provisions. (Again, you should verify that none of the following provisions are violative of your state's law.)

—"The contingency upon which compensation is to be paid is: (Specify contingency.)"

—"The Client is not to be liable to pay the Attorney compensation other than from the amounts collected for the Client by the Attorney, except as follows: (Specify circumstances, if any, which would obligate the Client to compensate the Attorney from monies other than amounts collected on behalf of the Client by the Attorney.)"

—"The Client is responsible for reasonable expenses and disbursements; provided, however, that no amount exceeding $200 will be advanced by the Attorney on behalf of the Client without prior consent of the Client. It is further agreed and understood that should the Client prevail

SAMPLE ATTORNEY-CLIENT AGREEMENT

This agreement is entered into by and between ____________________ ("Attorney") and ____________________ ("Client").

Attorney will perform the following services for Client:

(Here specify the services to be performed.)

Attorney estimates that legal services required by the Client will take approximately __________ to __________ hours and cost between __________ and __________ as follows:

(Here the lawyer lists hours and costs for handling different aspects of the case should certain variables occur.)

Disbursement costs (filing fees, deposition and transcript costs, transportation, etc.) will be paid by the Client. Attorney estimates that disbursement costs will be as follows:

(Here the lawyer itemizes possible disbursement costs.)

Prior to undertaking work beyond that initially specified, Attorney will provide Client with a written estimate of the additional time, fees, and disbursements involved and receive written permission from Client to undertake the work.

Attorney agrees to explain the laws pertinent to Client's problems, the available courses of action, and the attendant risks.

Attorney agrees to notify Client promptly of any significant development and consult with Client in advance on any significant decisions.

Attorney agrees to send Client a copy of all pertinent written materials sent or received by Attorney pertaining to Client's case. Client agrees to reimburse Attorney out-of-pocket costs for the reproduction of those materials.

/ Or: /

Attorney agrees to make available to Client for reading in Attorney's office all written materials sent or received by Attorney pertaining to Client's case. At Client's request, Attorney will provide copy of any material to Client at Attorney's out-of-pocket costs.

Attorney agrees to make all reasonable efforts to answer Client's inquiries promptly.

Client agrees to pay Attorney as follows:

(Here describe agreed upon fee arrangement.)

Client may terminate this agreement, with or without cause, upon written notice to Attorney. Attorney shall return Client's file immediately upon Client's terminating this agreement. Termination shall not affect Client's responsibility to pay for legal services rendered up to the date of termination. Attorney may terminate this agreement for reasons permitted under the __________ (state) Code of Professional Responsibility.

Nothing herein contained shall be interpreted to limit or restrict the Attorney's professional obligations under __________ (state) Bar's code or canons.

Dated:

____

Attorney

____

Client

or accept a settlement offer, the Client will be reimbursed the amounts expended for expenses and disbursements and the amount owed to the Attorney in fees will be deducted from the remainder."

—"In the event that the foregoing specified contingency occurs, the amount the Attorney is to be compensated shall not exceed the following maximum percentage of the gross amount collected less costs and expenses:

(Insert either a maximum percentage to be charged in the event of a recovery or a descending scale as agreed upon by the Attorney such as the following:

x% if settlement is secured prior to filing a suit;
x% if settlement is achieved after filing but before a trial has commenced;
x% if settlement occurs after the trial begins;
x% if an appeal is taken by the opposing party;
x% if the Client elects to take an appeal.)"

/OR:/

"In the event that the foregoing specified contingency occurs, the amount the Attorney shall be compensated shall not exceed the following percentages of the gross amount collected less costs and expenses:

x% of the first $50,000 of recovery;
x% of the next $25,000 of recovery;
x% of amounts recovered from $75,000 to $100,000;
x% of any amounts recovered in excess of $100,000."

/OR:/

"The Attorney has agreed to accept \$x as a flat fee in compensation for his representation provided however that if the Client recovers in excess of \$y, the Attorney is entitled to z% of the recovery on any amounts in excess of \$y in addition to the foregoing flat fee."

—"If the Attorney is discharged by the Client prior to the conclusion of the case or representation, the Attorney is entitled to reasonable expenses and disbursements up to and including the date of his or her discharge; the Attorney is also entitled to compensation for the value of his or her services up to and including the date of the discharge, not owed until the subject matter litigation is concluded in favor of the Client."

While the foregoing examples of contract terms cover the essential elements that should be contained in an attorney-client agreement, a person who is interested in preparing his or her own agreement should contact the state bar association to determine if they have sample forms that could be used. Most bar associations do not make such materials available, but this is beginning to change. Massachusetts, for example, does provide sample forms, and Florida will refer persons to a form book that they recommend as helpful. The important thing to keep in mind is that your contract must express all the details of the arrangement you reach with your attorney. Try to anticipate sore spots and provide solutions in the agreement.

OFFICE PROCEDURES

Once the attorney-client agreement is in place, the next most valuable thing a client can do is to learn how the office works. No matter what the size of the firm, every lawyer has help with the voluminous paperwork that flows in and out like the tide. A client should assess who is in charge of the day-to-day operations and deals with emergencies when the lawyer is in court or otherwise out of the office. Identify the person who makes the appointments, handles the banking, oversees the secretaries, arranges transportation, and keeps total chaos from breaking out. In small firms, this is usually the office manager or the secretary to the senior partner. This is a valuable person to get to know.

Once he or she has been singled out of the crowd, you should seek an introduction. It is nice, if not essential, to have another key person in the firm know your name and face. If in the weeks to come you experience difficulty in reaching the attorney or in receiving paperwork on time or in understanding the firm's bills, recourse is available.

❖

CHAPTER SEVEN

Bills

IN THE YEARS before the consumer movement took hold, the legal profession enjoyed a sense of security and autonomy from the close scrutiny of clients. Once a lawyer was employed, his activities were rarely questioned; the balance of power had shifted from that of a person with a problem to a client grateful for help. Today, bargaining positions are more equal, and an absence of accountability is unacceptable. A lawyer's bill is the most important record a client has to establish accountability.

THE COMPONENTS OF A BILL

If the attorney-client agreement clearly establishes the right to an itemized bill on a regular basis, it is all one should need to monitor and assess the progress of the case. In order to make sure you are getting your money's worth, a bill must detail exactly what work has been accomplished, by whom, and at what cost. This is true even if your case is being handled on

October 1, 1985
Mr. or Ms. Client
Address
Re: Purchase of Residence, High Ridge, New Jersey ①

For Services Rendered from September 1, 1985 to date: ②

9/1	SP	Negotiation with seller as to purchase price and fixtures to remain in house. ③	2.0⑤	@ $120	$240. ⑥
9/3	AS④	Inspection reports ordered for potability, termite and septic.	0.5	@ $75	$ 37.50
9/6	AS	Contract of sale and deed prepared.	1.5	@ $75	$112.50
9/7	SP	Review of bank commitment papers, contract and deed; contract signed pending outcome of inspection reports.	0.5	@ $120	$ 60.
9/8	AS	Survey reviewed; advice on title insurance and homeowners policy given; inspection reports obtained and reviewed.	1.0	@ $75	$ 75.
9/9	SP	Closing	1.0	@ $120	$120.
9/9	PL	Verification of filing of documents with city registries.	2.0	@ $20	$ 40.

Disbursements: Copying Costs . . . . $ 10. ⑦
Inspection Fees . . . . $ 35.
Survey . . . . $ 40.
Total Fees & Disbursements . . . . $770. ⑧

a contingency basis where you are obligated to pay only the costs of the action, and not fees. Without an itemized, monthly billing, you will be unable to track the progress of the case, and more importantly, you will have no basis for deciding how much, if anything, your attorney is owed if he is discharged or needs to withdraw from the representation at some point in the future.

The above is representative of the type of bill that should be generated where the attorney and client have agreed to an hourly fee structure.

Admittedly, a bill this detailed is exemplary. Analysis of

its component parts, however, should illustrate the kind of record keeping one has a right to expect from a lawyer.

1. *Account Name:* Frequently, a client has more than one account at the firm. Each matter is distinct and should be billed separately. Separate billing allows you to monitor the progress of each interest entrusted to the lawyer.

2. *Billing Period:* Every bill should reflect the specific time period of the work being invoiced.

3. *Activities Performed:* It is no longer necessary to tolerate a bill on embossed stationery that reads, simply: "In Re Jones: For Services Rendered . . . $1500." A lawyer performs a variety of services, some more productive than others. Each activity along with what was accomplished should be briefly summarized.

4. *The Person Who Performed the Work:* These initials reflect the name of the person who performed the identified service. In studying this bill, a client should be delighted that the less experienced associate was charged with the responsibility of ordering and reviewing reports, drafting the paperwork, and presumably making note of anything amiss that should be brought to the attention of the partner. Similarly, the client should be pleased to notice that the firm sent a paralegal to stand in line at the registry where such documents are recorded. The senior partner's time was spent negotiating, reviewing the financing arrangements, and signing up the deal. The allocation of the tedious chores to the less expensive associate and paralegal was a good use of resources.

5. *Time Expenditure:* A two-hour conference with the seller is a sizable block of time. A client reading this bill might be prompted to ask what was accomplished during this meeting.

6. *Rate and Charge:* The rate differences between a paralegal, an associate, and a partner are cost savings that should be passed on to the client.

7. *Costs and Disbursements:* The out-of-pocket, or ancillary, costs of a case should be itemized separately for a client's review.

8. *Total Owed:* As noted earlier, this hypothetical bill presumes that the attorney and the client agreed to an hourly fee basis. Although he got a good price for the services, if the client had explored the possibility of a flat fee, he might have come out ahead. Where a case is handled on a flat fee, percentage, or contingency basis, the total amount owed would not be included until the case is finished.

REVIEWING THE BILL

A carefully drafted attorney-client agreement is a valuable tool when it comes to reviewing a bill. If the agreement clearly specifies the services the attorney agreed to provide, the range of costs, and the form of the bill, the unpleasant task of calling an attorney to account for his charges is made all the easier. Irrespective of whether you entered into an attorney-client agreement, however, every client is well within his or her rights to question a bill that seems entirely too high. Bear in mind, though, that argument for argument's sake is counterproductive. Unnecessary confrontation and nit-picking at small annoyances will in the long run work to your detriment. No lawyer thinks highly of a client who is looking over his shoulder, questioning every expenditure, cramping his style. While every bill should be reviewed carefully and thoroughly, choose your battles prudently.

Although you should keep these words of caution in mind, there are two circumstances that justify speaking up: excessive charges and poor performance. In either case, you are completely within your rights to refrain from paying the bill until your concerns are satisfied. The difficulty, of course, is in recognizing overpriced services or a shoddy job when you see it.

Excessive charges: How can a layperson decide if the fee charged is excessive? Lawyers themselves have had a difficult time defining this concept. The Model Code of Professional Responsibility, drafted by lawyers for lawyers, provides that a fee "is clearly excessive when, after a review of the facts, a lawyer of ordinary prudence would be left with a definite and firm conviction that the fee is in excess of a reasonable fee." Hardly a useful measure. Perhaps a more workable definition is as follows: An excessive fee is one where the charges are inadequately detailed or are reflective of unproductive, unauthorized, or unnecessary work. Let's consider each of these possibilities.

Inadequately explained charges are easy to spot if you have insisted on an itemized bill. Any charge that is not detailed should be questioned. It may be that the attorney felt that the charge was self-explanatory. It may also be possible that he or she is trying to cover up mistakes.

Unproductive work is also fairly obvious. A lawyer who spends forever and a day "looking into" your problem is probably not leveling with you. Similarly, a lawyer who spends a week in settlement talks and ends up with a more polarized situation has been unproductive and possibly counterproductive. A client should find out just what the lawyer had hoped to gain and why he or she did not spend this time preparing for trial. While it is unrealistic to expect that every hour a lawyer spends will be productive, whole blocks of misdirected time should cause you concern.

Similarly, it is not too difficult to spot a charge for work one never requested. For example, if one is a writer and delivers a manuscript to an attorney with the instruction that all defamatory passages are to be noted in a short advisory opinion and the lawyer returns with a 120-page opus covering the waterfront on libel, the author is completely within his or her rights to refuse to pay for the unauthorized labor, however thorough and intelligent it may be.

Unnecessary labor is the most difficult to detect without a working knowledge of the law, and even then, great minds differ. Nevertheless, have confidence in the propriety of questioning disturbingly large charges. There really is no other recourse. If, for example, one spots a charge for fifteen hours of file organization performed by an associate, one may fairly question why a paralegal or a secretary was not assigned this housekeeping task. Similarly, an associate who is asked to come up with the answer to a narrow, discrete question but spends days in the library learning the field before the research question is even addressed no doubt has billed an outrageous time expenditure. The firm, and not the client, should bear the expense of the associate's scholarly initiation.

Poor performance: Apart from excessive costs, a client is equally within his or her rights to question a bill where one feels that an all-around poor job is being done with the matter. It is difficult of course to distinguish between a miserable case and a miserable effort. It may be that the lawyer has done all that can be done under the circumstances. Then again, you might be correct in your feeling that the lawyer's performance simply does not measure up to his fees. If you are troubled by the development of the case, it is appropriate to have a frank discussion about how your affairs are being managed. If months have gone by and the attorney appears to be no closer to understanding let alone resolving your problem but has been steadily billing you just the same, something is wrong and you should make your discontent known.

DISPUTING THE BILL

If the bill is problematic, do not pay it, and take the time to note each objection in writing. You should then arrange a face-to-face meeting with the attorney, which should be provided at no cost, for the specific purpose of discussing the problem charges. A telephone conversation is not adequate to demonstrate your concern. More important, it is easier to reach a compromise in person than over the phone.

When your meeting comes about, get straight to the point. Identify each of the troublesome charges and then ask the attorney to explain each item, point by point. With luck, a compromise might be reached. If such is the case, request that a revised bill be prepared and sent to your attention. If the new bill accurately reflects the compromise you reached, it should be paid promptly and in full. On the other hand, if the attorney has no reasonable explanation for the high costs and is unwilling to budge, inform him of your desire to seek a second opinion before you continue your discussion. Second opinions can be garnered from senior partners in the firm, other lawyers whom you may know, or outside financial consultants. If the consensus is that the bill is inflated but the attorney still refuses to see the error of his ways, two alternatives remain: Submit the matter to arbitration or sue. Both alternatives are unfortunate.

Arbitration: Arbitration is a quasijudicial procedure whereby the parties agree to place their dispute before an impartial person or panel who will hear both sides and render a final opinion. Over half the state bar associations and roughly two-thirds of the local bar associations provide some form of arbitration or grievance panel where attorneys and clients can voluntarily bring their fee disputes for resolution. As a general rule, sophisticated, hair-splitting lawyering is not tolerated during arbitration. A less formal and more private proceeding, arbitration is not intended as a forum for sorting out winners and losers but as a means for finding a common ground and reaching a compromise. The arbitrator is not bound by the rules of evidence, or indeed, by the law—an arbitrator can place more weight on the equities of the situation than on the technical requirements of the black letter law. In some states, the arbitrator is not even required to recite the reasons for his decision.

While it sounds attractive, be forewarned that the effectiveness of the proceeding varies from place to place. Many of these panels are staffed with other lawyers who at times display a disturbing reluctance to criticize a fellow member of the bar. Except in the most extreme and egregious cases, lawyers are averse to informing their colleagues that the bill is too high or the services do not merit the cost. The unwritten rule in some proceedings may well be: "Do unto others as you would have others do unto you." Adding to the difficulties with arbitration is the fact that with very few exceptions, the decision of the board is *final*—no appeals, the end.

Despite these drawbacks, if one concludes that an arbitrated grievance procedure is the best recourse, some effort should be made to learn as much as possible about the proceedings before submitting the problem. The bar association should be able to provide answers to the following questions: Are there any nonlawyers on the panel? Are there costs involved in initiating a proceeding? Are there rules of procedure, and if so, how may a copy be obtained? Is the decision of the board final? Is it possible to preserve a right of appeal? How soon can the matter be heard? Will a record of the proceeding be kept?

The answers to these questions can help one to determine if it is worth the effort to proceed in this fashion. If so, you should carefully prepare an argument and gather all the pertinent documents that support your claim of the unreasonableness of the fee. As a practical matter, without an attorney-client agreement that discusses the range of costs contemplated for the work, the chances of success are extremely slim. (The one exception to this would be in the circumstance where the attorney is asking for a contingency fee. In the absence of an agreement specifying a contingent arrangement, the attorney will be precluded from claiming the same after the case is concluded.)

It is also worth your while to give some thought to how much you are willing to compromise. Even if the arbitration panel is sympathetic to your complaint, it is unlikely that they will endorse your position 100 percent of the way. If you are asked how much you are willing to pay, you should be prepared to demonstrate some flexibility. It is to your advantage to impress the panel with your desire to be fair.

A lawsuit: In lieu of arbitration and in a case where a great deal of money is at stake, you could consider bringing a lawsuit against the attorney (see Chapter 10). Unlike arbitration, courts have become increasingly sensitive to the outrageous fees some attorneys charge, and in recent years, judges are finding the courage to slash monumental bills back down to human proportions. This necessitates firing the lawyer and hiring a replacement, of course, but in exceptional cases the expense and trouble may be worth it.

As a practical matter, no attorney will be pleased to hear that a client is contemplating a lawsuit against him. Defending a lawsuit is public, expensive, and time-consuming. It also blemishes a reputation (even if the attorney is ultimately successful) and makes other clients nervous.

INABILITY TO PAY

Brief mention should be made of the circumstance where the bill is completely justifiable, but the client is unable to pay. Mention of this subject is brief because one's alternatives are few. If you are in this jam, the first thing to do is to put a halt to all future work, no matter how pressing. Thereafter, arrange a meeting with the lawyer to discuss whether a settlement could be forced, if there is a way to cut down the amount of work necessary to complete the matter, or if the fee and/or payment terms could be renegotiated. If none of these alternatives is possible, the only choice remaining is to change counsel and find a lawyer you can afford.

❖

CHAPTER EIGHT

Living with Your Decision: The Attorney-Client Relationship

THE ATTORNEY-CLIENT relationship, like all important alliances in one's life, requires careful tending if it is to thrive and remain valuable. Both the attorney and the client must value and respect the association. An understanding of the rights and expectations of each party will strengthen the rapport and bode well for the future.

THE RESPONSIBILITIES OF AN ATTORNEY

The practice of law carries with it certain obligations. In an effort to consolidate and analyze each of these responsibilities, the American Bar Association studied the relationship between an attorney and a client, and released, in 1969, the

Model Code of Professional Responsibility. Their findings were organized into three interrelated parts: "canons," which set forth in general terms the standards of professional conduct that lawyers are expected to follow; "ethical considerations," which are aspirational objectives; and "disciplinary rules," which are mandatory provisions, the violation of which will give rise to sanctions. The model code served as a discussion paper for each of the state bar associations and legislatures. Within a few years of its release, each state adopted the code either in its entirety or with select revisions.

In 1983, the ABA altered the model code to take into account new rulings affecting, among other points, the law on conflicts of interest, advertising, minimum fee schedules, confidentiality, solicitation, and nonlawyer ownership of law firms. The result is a much more comprehensive set of ethical guidelines that is sensitive to the various roles a lawyer plays—representative, advisor, advocate, negotiator, intermediary, and expert. The new proposal, titled the Model Rules of Professional Conduct, also restructured the format of the material, eliminating the cumbersome tripartite division and consolidating the findings and interpretations into a more workable text. The draft is now circulating among the states, and it is expected that within the next few years, the proposal will be adopted either in its entirety or with some revisions in place of the model code. Until its adoption, however, the Model Code of Professional Responsibility sets the boundaries of ethical professional behavior.

Our discussion of the responsibilities and obligations of lawyers will be based largely upon the principles contained in the model code. In areas where the code provisions are dramatically changed or arguably unconstitutional in light of more recent opinions from the courts, however, the current thinking will be noted.

Drafted by lawyers for lawyers, the model code is as you

might expect a lengthy, technical, and at times tedious document. As such, it is not the kind of thing you should plan on reading. Cutting down to the essentials, a client has a right to expect seven things from his or her attorney: confidentiality, competence, loyalty, honesty and integrity, advocacy, counseling, and well-developed channels of communication. These seven points constitute the barest minimum acceptable professional behavior.

Confidentiality: A critical condition for effective representation is trust in your lawyer and honest communication. An attorney is incapable of adequately protecting a client's interests unless he or she is made privy to every fact, motive, objective, act, and concern of the client no matter how embarrassing, awkward, or awful it may be. To encourage the free flow of information, every state recognizes an obligation on the part of the attorney and his staff to preserve the secrets and confidences of clients as well as of prospective clients (that is, persons who interview the lawyer but do not elect to hire him).

To appreciate what an attorney does and does not owe you in terms of keeping your confidences, a quick lesson in the law is necessary. The principle of confidentiality is applied in two separate but related ways: the doctrine of confidences and secrets, which is a rule of ethics; and the attorney-client privilege, which is a rule of evidence. Let us consider each.

The ethical obligation requires an attorney to refrain from revealing your confidences and all sensitive matters regarding your representation. The obligation not only prevents him from disclosing such matters but prohibits him from using confidential information to his own advantage (in most circumstances) or to your disadvantage. What's more, even after an attorney and a client part ways, be it through the completion of the matter, discharge, or withdrawal of the attorney, the obligation to preserve confidences survives and continues. This, in essence, is the *ethical* component of confidentiality. While it may seem like pretty comprehensive protection, there are a number of exceptions that substantially undercut its effectiveness, which we will discuss momentarily.

The evidentiary component of confidentiality, termed the attorney-client privilege, comes into play when there is a judicial, tribunal, or other legal proceeding during which a lawyer may be called as a witness or otherwise compelled to produce evidence that concerns a client. Thus, it is compulsion of law that is involved here and not just an attorney's professional code of ethics. The attorney-client privilege holds that confidences falling under the umbrella of the privilege will be protected from compelled disclosure. To appreciate the kinds of communications that fall under the umbrella, one has to start from the basic premise that not everything a client regards as confidential is deemed confidential insofar as the law is concerned. It is important for a client to be able to differentiate between two kinds of statements: confidential remarks that are "privileged" (and therefore protected from disclosure), and confidential remarks that are outside the realm of the privilege (and therefore potentially subject to disclosure). The difference between these two kinds of communications depends largely upon the reasons why you hired the attorney and the circumstances during which the statement was made.

Let's first consider the scope of the employment. The rule is that communications pertaining to matters outside the scope of employment are not within the attorney-client privilege. If, for example, a client hires an attorney to incorporate a business and mentions in passing the trouble she is having with her spouse, the attorney's advice and their discussion of her marital woes are not privileged communications. Though the client may have regarded their conversation as private and confidential, family problems have nothing to do with the start-up of her business. The scope of the employment was corporate work, not domestic relations. While *ethically* the lawyer may be bound to keep her secrets, *legally* he could be forced to disclose the statements (say, for example, if he was asked to answer questions in connection with a subsequent divorce action).

As noted above, the setting of one's communications also comes into play with respect to the attorney-client privilege. Statements made to your lawyer in the presence of a person who is not a member of the attorney's staff or hired by the attorney to assist in the case are not deemed privileged communications. By allowing your thoughts to be aired in such a setting, you have lost your right to claim them as confidential. Likewise, letters or other written communications that are shown to persons outside the legal team are not as a general rule protected by the privilege. While there are exceptions, if you want a matter to remain confidential, it should be shared only with your attorney and people with whom he authorized you to speak.

Though you may now understand that not everything you confide is considered a confidential communication from an evidentiary point of view, you must still reckon with the ethical component of this problem before you can fully appreciate the limitations of an attorney's responsibilities to keep your confidences. Assuming you have a true confidential communication insofar as the attorney-client privilege is concerned, there are still five exceptions to the general *ethical* obligation that prohibits an attorney from breaching a confidence.

In the first of these exceptions, the attorney is allowed to disclose a confidence where in his discretion, he believes that he cannot adequately represent a client's interests without revealing the private information (as would be the case, for example, when an attorney decides to admit a fact that could not be properly disputed). Closely related is the second exception, which holds that the attorney may reveal the confidence when he or she convinces the client that it is in the client's best interests to do so and the client agrees. As such, the first two exceptions to the ethical rule appear to favor the client.

The next two exceptions work to the advantage of the attorney. He or she is authorized to reveal a confidence when it is necessary to establish a claim or defense on behalf of the lawyer as against the client—such as in the circumstance where the attorney is trying to collect an unpaid fee—or where it is necessary for the lawyer to protect himself or his staff against a claim of wrongful misconduct. (The model rules add that a confidence may be disclosed in a suit against the lawyer based on conduct in which the client was involved or to answer allegations regarding the lawyer's representation of the client.) The point here is that an attorney will keep your confidences so long as it does not require him to sacrifice his own interests to your cause.

The remaining exception favors neither the client nor the lawyer but is designed to advance the purposes of the criminal justice system. It is, simply, that the attorney is required to breach a confidence where it is necessary to prevent the commission of a criminal act. (The model rules narrow this exception to a certain kind of crime by providing that the attorney must believe that the criminal act is likely to result in imminent death or substantial bodily harm.) Note the future tense. The confession of misdeeds committed in the past are not matters that the attorney, as an officer of the court, must reveal. As such, tales of your past crimes may be safe, but discussion of future crimes puts you on shaky ground.

In view of the limitations of the attorney-client privilege and with five exceptions to the ethical rule, some in favor of you and others in spite of you, one may wonder whether the obligation to preserve secrets and confidences is worth much.

It is a fair question, and there is a real danger that your statements will slip through the cracks. The best advice is to proceed cautiously but not so timidly that you undercut your chances for effective representation. At times, it can be a fine balance, and each must find his or her own way.

Competence: Both the model code and the model rules provide that clients have a right to competent counsel. This sounds good, but precisely what it means is the subject of tremendous disagreement. Scholarly works that have grappled with the issue of how legal competence can be defined and measured have concluded that the question is still in its infancy, particularly as compared to other professions such as medicine.

Not the least of the problems in attempting to get at the heart of competence is the fact that the attorney-client privilege prevents the academic world from conducting an in-depth analysis of how cases are handled and whether the attorney has done the best job under the circumstances.

Nor can competence be measured by ethical considerations—in the eyes of the law, it is ethical, for example, for a lawyer to pursue his client's cause to the detriment of innocent persons or the good of society as a whole; it is ethical for a defense lawyer to bring forth information that is damaging to his client; it is ethical for a lawyer to accept a case even where he believes the client to be in the wrong; and it is ethical for a lawyer to manipulate facts so as to present them in an argumentative fashion calculated to advance the best interests of the client.

Other efforts at defining and measuring competence have been stymied at the realization that even the best lawyers are only as competent as the system that gives rise to lawyering. While I happen to agree with this observation, it does complicate matters. To adopt this approach requires that one first define the purposes of the justice system (about which there will always be great philosophical tugs-of-war) before one can turn to the question of measuring individual lawyer competence. And even if it is possible to reach a consensus on the purposes of the justice system, there will still be disagreement over the question of competent lawyering.

To illustrate this point, let us postulate that the goal of the justice system is to promote the just, parsimonious, and speedy resolution of disputes. In theory, a competent lawyer is one who acts in accordance with this goal. Must we conclude then that a lawyer who uses litigation as a stalling technique is incompetent? How about a lawyer who advances a technical argument as a "red herring"—is he incompetent? In neither of these instances is the lawyer acting in accord with our stated purposes of the justice system, yet to the client involved, the lawyer would probably appear to be extremely able and shrewd.

Elusive though the concept may be, however, there are some elementary observations about competence that can be made. At a minimum, certainly, competence requires technical knowledge, skill, thorough preparation, and cost-effectiveness. It also requires, I believe, that the attorney be physically, emotionally, and intellectually sound throughout the entire representation.

A competent attorney does not, however, necessarily possess a brilliant mind, incisive analytical skills, or boundless stamina. Nor does competence promise sound judgment, a strong network in the community, motivation, and an obsessive attention to detail. These things are extra. It is also important to realize that an attorney can be competent and still make mistakes, ranging from minor matters (such as miscalculations or filing errors) all the way to subtle but devastating strategic errors (such as a poorly conceived argument or hasty decision to waive a jury).

So what does this right to competent counsel amount to for the consumer of legal services? It means, in essence, that one is entitled to a lawyer who can lay claim to little more than basic skill, intelligence, and a respectable manner. And though an attorney may possess these attributes, which if taken together can be thought of as an underlying ability to perform, a client's right to competent counsel does not guarantee that an attorney will be attentive and careful in his case.

Loyalty: It is a cardinal principle that every client has the right to a full and undivided representation of his or her interests. Single-minded dedication and independent judgment are part of the service one can properly expect. If the attorney has a conflict of interest that causes his judgment to be affected or comprises his loyalty, steps need to be taken to rectify the situation. No one can serve two masters where the interests are antagonistic.

Conflicts of interest can arise in a variety of ways. The most common "conflicts" situation occurs when the attorney represents two different clients, in the same or substantially similar matter, whose interests conflict. Even if the representation of one of these clients has been concluded, the fact that the attorney has had close contact and inside knowledge of that client's affairs disqualifies him from representing new clients where the interests are adverse. The reason for the rule is plain: A client's interests cannot be adequately protected if the attorney is committed (or has been committed in the past) to looking out for the other person.

The same prohibition applies if the conflict situation arises with another lawyer in the firm. In this circumstance, even though the client and the client's opponent have separate counsel, the fact that both lawyers are members of the same firm raises the problem.

The important thing to focus on here is that the prohibition against the representation of conflicting interests is triggered only where the same case or a closely related case is involved. As such, a lawyer is barred, for example, from trying to rescind on behalf of one client a contract he drafted for a former client. It is not a conflict of interest, however, for an attorney to represent a client and a major competitor of the client if he is handling completely unrelated problems for each and if there is no danger of confidential information supplied by one party being used to the detriment of either. Similarly, it is not a conflict (though it may well be bad taste) for an attorney to be representing a client today for one thing and months later be suing him in connection with an unrelated matter. Sorting out who represented whom, when, and for what reason can be such a massive and intricate task that the larger firms have taken to computerizing this information.

The moment an attorney realizes that he has a conflict-of-interest problem, one of three options is available: First, he can inform all the parties of the problem as well as of the potential consequences and obtain a written consent from each as to his continued representation of everyone; second, he can withdraw from the representation of all but one of the parties after he has informed everyone of the situation; or finally, he can totally withdraw from the representation of everyone. (Some lawyers claim that they are forced to turn down more cases than they accept as a result of the conflict-of-interest rule.)

If the conflict appears elsewhere in the firm, some practitioners try to isolate the conflicting attorney from any participation in the new matter, which includes hearing of or reading any pertinent information. In the trade, this solution is often referred to as "building a Chinese wall." While this practice goes on, it is not always honored by the courts as a sufficient remedy to the problem. Indeed, some courts have gone so far as to say that not only is every member of the firm disqualified, but even attorneys who are not part of the same firm but merely share office space are prohibited from participating in the case.

There are other types of conflicts of interest that can arise. An attorney may have a political, religious, or philosophical belief that prevents him from giving a case his full allegiance. Similarly, the conflicts problem can surface when the attorney has a personal interest in his client's affairs and is no longer capable of separating his private feeling from his professional advice. It is likewise a conflict for an attorney to possess a financial stake in his client's ventures if his ability to render impartial assistance is impaired. As tempting as it may first appear, enlisting your attorney as a business partner is not a good idea. It requires that the attorney wear two hats—that of an independent advisor and that of an interested party. Despite the many dangers posed, however, it is popular these days for law firms to be investing in start-up companies on par with prominent venture capitalists. Be wary of this kind of enthusiasm, and seek your backing elsewhere.

No matter how the conflict of interest arises, the client can never be fully confident that the attorney is exercising independent judgment on his behalf, and steps should be taken to rectify or terminate the relationship. If you learn of a potential conflict, discuss the matter with your attorney and ask that he or she put a full explanation in writing. If in the weeks to come a question is raised as to the propriety of the continued representation, it is the attorney who must bear the burden of demonstrating that his decision was reasonable.

Honesty and integrity: An attorney is a fiduciary, which means that he or she is required to act with the highest degree of honesty, integrity, and candor. A client must be comfortable with the notion that his or her attorney is completely trustworthy. Trust is what compensates for the unequal balance of power between lawyer and layperson.

While trust can be abused on many levels, the most frequent problems occur over money. Oftentimes, an attorney is invested with a large sum to hold on behalf of a client. The duty of honesty and integrity requires that such funds be kept in a separate, interest-bearing account to assure that the money will not lose its separate ownership. The danger is that commingled funds may be used for the attorney's personal expenses or subjected to the claims of his creditors. The attorney should also provide periodic reports with respect to the activity of such funds. Indeed, the model rules go so far as to say that the records pertaining to such an account must be preserved for five full years following the termination of the representation.

If you cannot trust your attorney, for whatever reason or suspicion, you should immediately begin to seek other counsel (see Chapter 9).

Advocacy: As we have discussed earlier, many problems that come before a lawyer do not involve advocacy. A client who is in need of a will, basic financial advice, help with corporate documents, or assistance in the purchase of a home, for example, does not have an opponent per se. Other problems, however, involve heated and, at times, vicious debates. Family problems, labor relations, corporate battles, and government investigations provide a handful of illustrations where a forceful spokesperson is vital. It is with respect to these kinds of cases that a client's right to a vigorous, unequivocal, and partisan representation is triggered. Irrespective of what the attorney may think of the client or the cause, personal judgments should not stand in the way of confident advocacy. For better or worse, it is an essential feature to the design of our justice system.

Counseling: Apart from playing an *advocate,* a lawyer is also an *advisor.* These are two very different roles. As an advocate, a lawyer is forced to deal with the facts as he finds them—whatever has come and gone is water over the dam. As an advisor, he can shape the future, which gives the attorney far more latitude in handling your affairs. In rendering advice, he or she can look not only to the law but to moral, economic, social, and political considerations that may be relevant to your situation.

A good attorney will work hard to make available as many options as possible. His or her job is to lay out your alternatives and assist you in evaluating the relative merits of each. An attorney can venture an opinion, of course, but most critical decisions (such as whether to accept a settlement offer, waive a jury, or take the stand) are yours and yours alone unless you specifically defer to your attorney. And assuming your decisions are within the boundaries of the law, your wishes will be binding on your lawyer. Indeed, an attorney is barred from taking any action that would irrevocably prejudice a client's position or otherwise affect the merits of the case without first seeking his client's blessing.

Communication: An attorney bears the responsibility of creating and maintaining strong lines of communication with a client. This responsibility includes an obligation to explain the pertinent laws, to answer all questions, to keep a client informed about the progress of the work, and to allow the client access to the files and/or to provide copies of significant paperwork. In addition, implicit in this responsibility is the obligation to communicate in intelligible English.

Believe it or not, this is a tall order for a lot of attorneys. A lawyer who is pressed for time or who hasn't really thought the situation out may prefer to keep his clients in the dark.

Other lawyers, whether out of arrogance or insecurity, simply don't believe that clients have the right to know what's going on. With attitudes such as these, it will be up to the client to enforce his right to communication.

Every client should make it his business to obtain copies of all significant paperwork associated with the case (including, for example, substantive correspondence, pleadings, research memos, contracts, deeds, corporate papers, leases, tax statements, and agreements). A file should be set up at home or in one's office where such records can accumulate undisturbed. In addition to collecting these materials, you should read them and discuss anything you do not understand with your lawyer. While some of the material will be too technical to comprehend, it is a rare client who is unable to perceive the drift of things, and your perceptions may trigger a consideration or strategy the attorney overlooked. The more active you are in a case, the more likely that it will be resolved to your satisfaction. Ineffective communication on the part of your attorney, however, will seriously hamper your ability to participate.

There is a second purpose to maintaining a file and actively participating in your case. If you and your attorney experience a difference of opinion that is so serious that you need to change counsel, your knowledge of the case coupled with your file of essential documents will provide tremendous assistance to your new attorney and preserve valuable time that is usually lost during such transitions.

THE RESPONSIBILITIES OF A CLIENT

Unlike a lawyer's obligations, the responsibilities of a client are not researched, carefully analyzed, or neatly set forth in a code or rule book. In the interest of promoting a strong professional relationship, however, some attention should be paid to the expectations a lawyer may have about his or her client. A successful, harmonious, and profitable alliance requires a mutual understanding.

Prompt payment: By placing the question of payment at the top of the list, I do not mean to suggest that a lawyer's profits are his or her most dominant concern. The truth is, however, that much of the disharmony between clients and lawyers turns on the question of money. While a carefully drafted attorney-client agreement goes a long way in heading off fee disputes, clients do get angry that the work isn't progressing fast enough or to their satisfaction, and as a result, they stop paying the bills. A lawyer has a basic right to be paid for his services and to be paid promptly. Even if you have decided to discharge the attorney, as a general proposition you are expected to compensate him up until the termination of the relationship (see Chapter 9).

Assistance: A lawyer expects assistance from a client, which includes answering all questions honestly, providing paperwork promptly, following instructions, and taking an interest in the case. It is extremely difficult, if not impossible, to work up enthusiasm for a client who habitually ignores what he was asked to do, withholds information, or misrepresents important facts. If you don't trust your lawyer enough to deal honestly with him, change counsel.

It is also important to assist your attorney in keeping sight of the goal. Only you know your own psychological and financial limits. Be alert for an expeditious and economical resolution. At times, you are better situated to spot a way out of the mess than is your attorney.

Realism: Attorneys are only human, despite what some of them would have you believe. They can work extremely hard, they can fight and even get lucky, but they are not sorcerers capable of moving heaven and earth at a client's behest. There are strong cases and miserable cases; winners and losers. If yours is a case your own mother wouldn't take pity on, the most you can hope for is to cut your losses.

Good behavior: No self-respecting lawyer will tolerate a pain-in-the-neck client. If you are prone to haranguing your attorney, arriving late for meetings, giving press statements without clearance, casting aspersions on professional competence, spreading calumnious charges, or engaging in other similarly distasteful behavior, do not be surprised if the lawyer withdraws from the representation. What's more, it is likely that word will get around, and efforts to replace the attorney could prove to be extremely difficult.

Gratitude: Most people enjoy a little praise now and again, and lawyers are no exception. While optimism and encouragement are appreciated, however, expensive gifts are (or should be) offensive. Though there is disagreement on the subject, expensive watches, shiny new briefcases, antiques, oil paintings, choice perfume, and fine Cuban cigars run counter to the concept of professionalism. It is as if the accompanying note read: "Hey counselor, I give expensive gifts. Put your other clients aside and pay more attention to me."

As a professional, the attorney should not require expensive gifts to focus his or her attention on the case. He is paid to be attentive, and that is compensation enough. If a client is moved to show gratitude above and beyond payment of the bill in full, and on time, he or she should wait until the conclusion of the case.

Following advice: Some clients simply can't resist the temptation to meddle in their own affairs and muck up the works. Dealing with lawyers is expensive, time-consuming, unsettling, and often aggravating. At the least, you should take the advice you pay for.

❖

CHAPTER NINE

When to Jump Ship

DESPITE the best efforts, sometimes things just don't appear to be working out as anticipated. You may feel that your work is being neglected or that your attorney is sloppy. Maybe the chemistry is simply not right. While unpleasant to contemplate, a persistent difference of opinion is enough to force a parting of the ways. Or possibly, you may be completely happy with your attorney but he is the victim of a sudden illness or emergency that requires his withdrawal.

Whatever the precipitating cause, you should be prepared to jump ship if the circumstances merit a change. This is rarely easy and often uncomfortable, but if you know what to expect, you can minimize your losses. The objective is to wrap up your deteriorating affairs in an expeditious but tidy manner, hire a capable replacement, and preserve your interests during the transition.

DISCHARGING AN ATTORNEY

Every client possesses a nearly absolute right to fire his or her lawyer—with or without cause, with or without a contract, no questions asked. Indeed, in all but the rare case where the aim is to obstruct, circumvent, or delay proceedings, an attorney can be discharged on a whim. An offensive habit, a repugnant cigar, an irritating demeanor, or the annoying liberty of adopting terms of endearment when addressing women are cause enough for some clients. Such unbridled power, however, should not be exercised capriciously.

It is neither comfortable nor economical to change counsel. The time involved is but one of the costs. There are also the problems of transferring the files, bringing the new attorney up to speed, establishing a rapport, developing a strategy, and assuring that the work proceeds without further delay. The timing of the change can pose other problems as well. If you are in the midst of sensitive dealings, a change of counsel could jeopardize any hard-earned ground. In the middle of a trial, a change could prove to be disastrous. All evidence comes to a standstill, the judge becomes impatient, and opposing counsel manages to work in a passing remark about the unfortunate inconvenience of it all.

TROUBLE SIGNS

Bother and prejudice notwithstanding, there is little one can do about an unmistakably bad attorney except seek a replacement. The difficulty, of course, is in deciding when enough is enough. In this regard, there are certain trouble signs, which, if spotted, should raise your eyebrows. If they persist, the matter must be taken in hand.

Serious mistakes: An attorney is usually up to his waist in detail. In the day-to-day thrashing about, sometimes important matters are mismanaged. No one is infallible; small mistakes, if infrequent, can and should be forgiven. Serious mistakes, however, deserve prompt attention. The difficulty lies in the detection. Short of schooling yourself in the technical intricacies of the law, the best recourse is to establish good channels of communication and monitor closely the attorney's activities, keeping an eye out for setbacks. Missing an important deadline, misconstruing the law, being unable to work amicably with opposing counsel, or showing bad judgment or unmitigated ignorance are all serious mistakes on the part of your attorney. Where your interests are or could be seriously jeopardized by them, it is time to consider a change of counsel.

Inattentiveness: There is no excuse for the failure to provide the requisite attention to a client's affairs. Unreturned phone calls, delays in answering correspondence, rushed meetings, general unavailability, all-around neglect, or the delegation of substantially all the work to a more junior person are indications of inattentiveness. When a client is left with the impression that his or her affairs are the farthest thing from the attorney's mind, it is time to reevaluate the situation.

Change in attitude: Once snared into the business fold, some clients experience a fall from grace. Maybe the attorney has received better, more important, more interesting, or more lucrative cases since he took on yours; maybe he misjudged what he thought he could do for you; or perhaps he has grown to dislike you. Whatever the cause, you may perceive that the attorney is no longer as courteous or as patient as he once was, that he puts you off, treats your questions with subtle indifference, or is out and out offensive. Shifts in attitude should not be ignored. Indiscretions and small discourtesies, if not checked, persist and proliferate. If the atmosphere has turned decidedly chilly, inquiries must be made.

Failure to follow instructions: A lawyer's scope of authority in the representation of your interests is by no means clear-cut. Certainly, *you* possess the ultimate authority to define the purpose of the representation; as long as your objectives are legal and reasonable, an attorney is bound to follow your wishes. At the same time, however, a lawyer bears the responsibility for technical and tactical decisions particularly (but not exclusively) where litigation is concerned. As such, a client-lawyer relationship is not technically that of an employer and an employee. A lawyer has an ethical obligation to exercise independent judgment, which may mean that he will not obey your every command. When he deviates from your expressed purposes and predominate objectives, however, a frank discussion is in order.

Misconduct: Intentionally errant (if not criminal) behavior is dangerous to a client's interests. The commingling of funds, a breach of confidence, and dishonesty or deceit of any magnitude are examples of the kind of misconduct that should motivate you to action. No excuse for this kind of behavior is sufficient. Whatever the reason for the transgression, your interests have been prejudiced if not irreparably harmed and you should be quick about finding other counsel.

The foregoing catalog of trouble signs is meant to delineate the demarcation between a healthy representation and one that has deteriorated. The five types of unacceptable behavior mentioned are where I draw the line. Each person must assess for himself, however, what constitutes the minimum standard of care. That standard firmly fixed in mind, you must resist the temptation to make excuses for deviant behavior or to let the transgressions slide. If a real problem is looming on the horizon, face it and take steps to resolve the difficulty.

ORCHESTRATING A SMOOTH TRANSITION

A decision to fire an attorney should not be arrived at lightly. To assure a reasoned judgment, there are three steps you should follow: First, confront the attorney and seek an explanation; second, weigh the alternatives; and finally, make your move.

Step 1. Confrontation: It is detrimental to the client as well as to the attorney-client relationship to let suspicious and troublesome irregularities pass unheeded. Despite this, clients are often reluctant to air their concerns due to a misplaced belief that either nothing can be done or criticism is likely to erode relations further. While it is true that a frank discussion with your attorney that dwells upon his or her shortcomings is likely to cause some discomfort, the alternative (doing nothing) is even more likely to result in an awkward end to the relationship.

At the first persistent signs of a serious problem, make an appointment to meet with the attorney and let him or her know that the purpose of your visit will be to evaluate performance. A face-to-face dialogue will underscore the importance of your doubts and foster better communication.

Begin the meeting by getting right to the point, but after you candidly identify your concerns, give the attorney an opportunity to respond. You may learn that the only real problem has been a lack of communication. Your information may be incorrect or you may be misinterpreting things. Then again, you may be correct about your misgivings. While you should allow him a chance to explain, it is inappropriate for him to suggest that you have blown things out of proportion or are behaving foolishly, and you should not accept this as a sufficient explanation for the problem.

Be careful at this juncture not to let the attorney know that you are thinking of changing counsel. Even if you are absolutely certain that a change is necessary, it is a grave error to voice this thinking until a replacement has been lined up. A new attorney can help you to preserve your interests during the transition and advise you on how to handle any loose ends. It is possible, of course, depending on the tenor of your conversation, that the attorney could threaten to quit (see "Withdrawal" below). If this is the case, you will have to expedite your efforts to hire a replacement. You may also have to remind the attorney that if he backs out and prejudices your interests in the process, he will surely have to answer to the disciplinary committee (see Chapter 10).

Step 2. Weighing the alternatives: In certain circumstances, your worst fears will be confirmed on the basis of the meeting with the attorney, and as such, it will be an easy matter to consider your alternatives. For example, if you strongly suspect that your attorney has been embezzling funds and you present him with your evidence, he or she may quickly admit the deed and offer to make restitution in the hopes of extracting a promise from you to forgo pressing criminal charges. In this circumstance, there really is no other alternative but to change counsel and press charges. A person who cheats you once cannot be trusted to behave honorably in the future.

Other situations may not be so clear-cut. If you complain that your work is being neglected and the attorney protests that three months is a normal amount of time for such matters, how can you be sure that he or she isn't exaggerating to cover for lax work habits? A phone call to a trusted friend, a law school professor, or a member of the bar association grievance committee may help you to assess your alternatives.

It may be possible to go above the attorney's head and speak with a more senior partner about having the case reassigned within the firm. Alternatively, perhaps a more senior person will speak with the errant attorney and straighten him out. If firing the attorney is the best recourse, however, do not let emotional hesitations cloud the picture. Despite clear indications that it is time to move on, some clients never get around to changing counsel for fear of making waves or creating an embarrassing situation. These fears are not justifiable reasons to keep from doing what is in your best interest.

Step 3. The move: This is an awkward time, and care should be taken to minimize your losses. As such, every effort should be made to part as amicably as the circumstances will allow. The new attorney should be involved in helping you through the transition period, which includes transferring records, settling the old account, developing a new strategy, and tending to odds and ends.

The most important matter to concentrate on at the outset is the transfer of your records to the new attorney. The Model Code of Professional Responsibility requires that the outgoing attorney forward all documents, working papers, memos, notes, research files, witness statements, and other written material as soon as possible. Despite an affirmative duty to minimize prejudice, however, some attorneys will drag their feet at this juncture on the pretense of having to organize the files or inventory the documents. If you have maintained your own file of important documents as advocated in prior chapters, copies of this file should be turned over to the new attorney at once.

An attorney who is slow to surrender vital paperwork is probably of the opinion that you owe him money. Indeed, he not only can stall but in most jurisdictions is legally authorized to impose a "retaining lien" on the paperwork. While the law governing retaining liens varies from state to state, in general it operates as a freeze on the transfer of valuable papers until the attorney is paid or there is a determination that no payment is owed. The retaining lien is a powerful leverage device to force an unwilling client to settle his bill. (A client who is unable, rather than unwilling, to pay has an easier chance of getting out from under the lien. Where the client is indigent or where a contingency arrangement was structured specifically to accommodate the client's insufficient financial resources, the courts are more inclined to set aside the lien and demand the transfer of documents.)

Just what, if anything, you owe the outgoing attorney—or what he or she owes you—can be a tricky question. Certainly any advance payments that have not been earned are to be returned. More frequently, however, it is the client who is in debt to the attorney. What is owed, though, depends upon why the attorney is being discharged. If he or she is being fired "without cause," you should expect to have to compensate him for the reasonable value of his services up until the date of the discharge. If fired "for cause," you owe him nothing. As should be immediately apparent, which acts constitute "cause" and which do not is usually the subject of sharp disagreement. As a rule of thumb, if the attorney's actions are serious enough to warrant the institution of a malpractice suit, whether or not you choose to go this route, you are probably safe in assuming that there is cause enough to fire him and no payment is owed. (See Chapter 10 for a discussion of malpractice.)

The question of what is owed is further complicated if the case was being handled on a contingency basis. If the client has not been adamant about an itemized billing, there is no guide for measuring the fair value of work done to date (see

Chapter 7). At this point, the attorney may insist that he be compensated on an hourly basis, which forces the client to accept his word on how many hours he has expended. It is also conceivable that the attorney will demand a percentage of the best settlement offer he has been able to secure thus far or that he will lay claim to a percentage of what the new attorney is able to win. None of these alternatives is favorable, but somehow a compromise must be fashioned.

Despite the many difficulties that could arise in settling the bill, your goal should be to dispense with this as quickly and quietly as possible. As such, you should be prepared to meet the attorney halfway and to accept a reasonable offer. Not only can he or she hold up records until the fee is settled, but it can be extremely difficult to get a new attorney to take the case on with the matter of fees outstanding. The new attorney will be fearful that his own compensation might be jeopardized, and ill will between you and your former attorney will hamper the new lawyer's efforts to learn the case. Not all of a lawyer's work is reduced to written form. Much of it is in impressions, insights, hunches, theories, educated guesswork, and strategy. The outgoing attorney's assistance in imparting his headwork to the new attorney can be quite valuable. If he chooses to, he can help familiarize the new attorney with the case by summarizing what has been done, what could have been done, and what had best be attended to, immediately. One way to encourage this kind of assistance is to bend a little on the issue of how much the outgoing attorney is owed.

While efforts should be directed at compromise, the client nevertheless may feel that the attorney is trying to take advantage of the situation and demand more than his fair share. Here the threat of a disciplinary action or a malpractice suit may bring the attorney to his senses. It may also be necessary to submit the fee dispute to an arbitration panel for resolution. Neither of these alternatives is desirable, however, since it is not a good idea to deplete your resources with a tangential battle. It is hard enough to change counsel without having to take on a separate fight over fees.

Once the fee question has been settled and the transfer of records completed, all that remains are a few loose ends. The first is to reduce to written form the substance of your agreement with the outgoing attorney. Take the time to draft a letter that details why you hired him, why you fired him, and the outgoing arrangements the two of you reached with respect to fees, files, and other forms of assistance. A copy of this letter should be retained in your personal files and the original sent by registered mail. In the event that you are sued for nonpayment of fees, this letter serves as a valuable record of the agreed-upon arrangement.

The other letter you should take the time to write is one to the disciplinary committee of the local bar association. Even though you may have no desire to file a complaint, a brief letter outlining the problems you experienced is further protection for you if the outgoing attorney decides to make trouble at a later date.

WITHDRAWAL

Even if you are delighted with your attorney, you still may be forced to find a replacement if your lawyer decides to withdraw from the representation. The Model Code of Professional Responsibility requires an attorney to withdraw where any of the following circumstances arise: The attorney has a conflict of interest that cannot be resolved; there is a physical or mental condition which renders him incapable of providing the requested service; the attorney learns that the main purpose for the case is to harass or maliciously injure another person; the attorney has been discharged; or finally, the attorney believes that continued representation will violate the Model Code of Professional Responsibility.

If any of the foregoing circumstances is present, an attorney's withdrawal from a case is mandatory. There are other circumstances, however, where withdrawal is voluntary and left to the discretion of the individual lawyer. The Model Code of Professional Responsibility cites ill health, lack of client cooperation, a client's desire to pursue an unwarranted or illegal course of action, failure of the client to meet his payment obligations, and the inability to get along as valid reasons that could justify a voluntary withdrawal. The model rules, however, provide far more leeway to attorneys in this regard and include factors such as financial hardship, the client's desire to pursue an objective the attorney regards as repugnant or imprudent, the failure of the client to follow instructions, the burdensomeness of the representation, or the catchall "for good cause."

Whatever the reason for the withdrawal, be it mandatory or voluntary, the attorney has a responsibility to do his best not to jeopardize your interests. Accordingly, he is required to give you due notice of his intentions and, if possible, to refer you to a new attorney and to cooperate with the new team. Cooperation is required even where the reason for the withdrawal is the nonpayment of fees. As a practical matter, however, cooperative efforts under such circumstances would be halfhearted at best.

As to the question of what is owed an attorney who withdraws, the answer is again that it depends upon the reason for the departure. If the client was the precipitating cause (as would be the case, for example, if the client insisted upon an illegal course of action), it is conceivable that he or she will be responsible not just for the value of services performed to date but for the whole fee. If the client was not the motivating factor, however, it is likely that only the value of the services performed to the date of withdrawal or some slightly lower amount will be owed.

❖

CHAPTER TEN

Disciplinary Actions and Malpractice Suits

SOMETIMES changing counsel is not enough. If the misconduct is serious, you may desire to pursue the matter one step further by bringing a disciplinary action against the lawyer, a malpractice suit, or both. While both proceedings are alternatives to standing by idly, it is important to ask yourself whether either avenue of redress is really worth the effort.

DISCIPLINARY PROCEEDINGS

The legal profession, like most professions, is charged with the responsibility of policing the activities of its own members. While at first blush this may strike you as a conflict of interest, the system is not unusual. The concept of self-regulation is a central feature in the definition of a profession and a recurring theme in the historical development of our conception of professionalism. The reasons for this are twofold: The first reason is that policymakers have traditionally believed that the demands of most professions are by definition too technical for the average layman to comprehend, and as such, there is little alternative but to leave the regulation of its members in the hands of the profession itself. The second and less palatable justification for the system was the sentiment that professionals were too educated and indeed too elite to have to tolerate the say-so of the common man over their affairs.

For decades, this power has translated into a guildlike monopoly over the delivery of legal services. And until recently, society has tolerated self-regulation on the assumption that the bar really is best suited to deal with wayward attorneys and that such an arrangement would serve to protect the average citizen from exploitation and incompetence.

Today, other professions, such as medicine, banking, and architecture, feel the hand of government regulation encroaching upon their once exclusive terrain. The legal profession too is being forced to surrender some of its authority as a result of burgeoning consumer awareness and pressure from corporate clientele who draw heavily upon legal services. The teaching of the 1970s for lawyers is that the bar's efforts toward self-regulation were perceived by the public as wholly inadequate. Widespread public dissatisfaction, triggered in large measure by a post-Watergate mentality, resulted in a demand for greater accountability among lawyers.

Bar associations, on national, state, and local levels, have responded to this call. Their rapid response was motivated both by a sincere desire to restore the profession as a whole to the elevated stature it once enjoyed as well as by a desire to act quickly in its own behalf, thereby short-circuiting government intervention (from the Federal Trade Commission among others), which many legal historians believe would otherwise have been inevitable. Nevertheless, the fact that it has taken so long to see lawyers turn toward seriously policing their own rank and file is testimony to the strength and political autonomy of the bar.

Regulating authorities: Technically speaking, the legal profession is regulated on a state-by-state basis with the primary responsibility vested in the auspices of the state supreme court. (The federal system is separate from this and imposes its own rules on those who elect to practice in this sphere.) As a practical matter, however, the state supreme court's control over the bar involves little more than sporadic rule-making and acting as the final arbiter in appeals from disciplinary actions. The real nitty-gritty of the authority is conferred by the courts to the state and local bar associations.

The bar's effort at governing its brethren is confined for all practical purposes to two groups: those who are allowed to enter the ranks and those who are permitted to stay. With respect to entrance requirements, prospective lawyers are required to complete three years of professional education, pass a bar exam that purports to test substantive knowledge, and survive an inquiry into the moral fitness and character of the applicant. The fitness exam usually consists of an interview where the bar examiner questions the applicant's lifestyle, values, affiliations, and attitude about the law.

The other area of the bar's regulatory efforts (i.e., those who are permitted to stay) focuses on the enforcement of the rules and norms of professional conduct. Opinions vary as to the effectiveness of this area of activity. The severest critics maintain that the state of discipline is a shocking disgrace. More charitable views acknowledge that professional discipline is an enormous and complicated task. Certainly one of the main difficulties is that while thousands upon thousands of complaints are brought per state each year, disciplinary efforts are confined to weeding out only the worst offenders, who are guilty of grossly unethical behavior. With respect to these malefactors, and particularly where they are prominent public figures, the bar rarely misses the opportunity to proclaim loudly the sanctions it meted out. More benign acts of negligence or incompetence, however, matters that touch the everyday lives of average citizens, are handled in private, and go largely unpunished.

The complaint process: Complaints against lawyers can be brought by other lawyers, judges, clients, and third parties adversely affected by the lawyer's conduct. As one might expect, the largest number of complaints is generated from clients. Lest one fear repercussions from a lawyer as a result of the complaint, it may be heartening to note that in the majority of states, a client cannot be sued by an attorney for the allegations in the complaint even if it is later determined that the attorney acted ethically.

The procedure for commencing a disciplinary action varies from state to state. In almost all jurisdictions, however, the process is begun by writing a letter to the Chief Counsel of the state or local bar association's committee on grievances. Every bar association has such a committee or panel although the name may vary from place to place (e.g., grievance committee, lawyer disciplinary committee, ethics committee). The letter should be short but factual and should state why the lawyer was retained; the substance of the problem; the relevant dates, dollar amounts, and other specifics; and the names, addresses, and phone numbers of the pertinent parties. Copies of any paperwork that is necessary or helpful in understanding the complaint should also be included. The letter should further request that the grievance committee investigate the matter, lodge a formal complaint against the lawyer, and keep the writer informed of any developments. Be sure you keep a copy for your files.

Care should be taken in presenting your views in a concise, organized, and logical manner. This is all the more important if you are complaining about a well-known, highly regarded member of the bar. A letter that omits pertinent facts, lacks cogency, or plays too heavily on emotional concerns is likely to be disregarded or discounted in view of the attorney involved. Every effort must be made to give the impression that the unhappy complainant is intelligent, articulate, and reasonable.

Upon receipt of the letter, the grievance committee will commence an investigation, which can take up to two months or more depending upon the backlog of cases in the office. As part of the investigation, the client as well as other persons referred to in the complaint can expect to be interviewed.

The committee has a number of options available to it, and the course it elects to follow will depend on the results of the investigation. If the complaint *does not* raise any ethical considerations, which is true of the vast majority of complaints filed, it will most likely be dismissed and the complainant so notified. (Among the more common examples are letters complaining about a judgment call that in hindsight turned out to be incorrect, a minor disagreement not attributable to misconduct, or the refusal of an attorney to accept a case.) Where the complaint *does* present an ethical problem, but a minor one (such as letters that complain about rude or insulting behavior), a committee member may phone the complainant to smooth over hurt feelings or may pressure the attorney to put forth his best efforts in reaching a compromise. If the committee concludes that the complaint is really in the nature of a contract dispute, such as a garden variety argument over fees, the complaint may be referred to an arbitration panel or other dispute settlement forum. Finally, where the committee makes a preliminary determination of unethical conduct (as would be the case, for example, with a fee that is illegal or unconscionably high), a copy of the complaint, or summary, will be sent to the lawyer for his or her response.

When a grievance committee calls, a lawyer pays attention. To ignore a request from it is in itself an act of misconduct. As such, you can be sure the lawyer will give his answer serious consideration, even if he thinks the charges are baseless or inconsequential.

In most states, if the lawyer's response does not resolve the matter, the committee then has the option of convening a hearing panel. In the old days, such panels were almost always composed of members of the grievance committee, who for the most part were other lawyers. This practice has been widely criticized. As a result, twenty-nine of the states now include nonlawyers on the committee.

The hearing panel has fairly broad investigatory powers. It can subpoena witnesses, ask to see documents, and consider any evidence it deems relevant to the proceedings. The attorney also has the prerogative of calling witnesses and presenting evidence on his own behalf. While the practice varies, most frequently the complainant is not entitled to be present at the disciplinary hearing but will be informed of the outcome. The proceedings are likewise closed to the public. This secrecy element, though criticized by legal commentators, does not end here. In most states, an attorney's disciplinary record, at least through this hearing stage of the complaint process, is not available to the general public. Moreover, in at least ten states, the grievance committee itself does not have access to information concerning prior offenses until there has been a finding of misconduct in the pending matter.

As a practical matter, the hearing panel is looking for two things: infractions of the state's criminal law and/or violations of the state's code of professional responsibility or ethical obligations. Most of the complaints considered by the panel allege wrongdoing in the course of the attorney-client relationship. In over forty states, however, the panel is entitled to pursue the matter whether or not the alleged misconduct occurred in connection with the lawyer's professional activities. In other words, the committee is authorized to investigate even where the charges concern a lawyer's actions while serving as a shareholder of a corporation, an attorney's activities as an officer or director of a corporation, alleged misconduct while acting in the capacity of a fiduciary, or even purely private conduct of the lawyer although this is rare.

While it depends upon the nature of the charges, as a general proposition, it will not do the attorney much good to argue, for example, that he made an honest mistake, he returned the stolen goods, he did not intend to profit, he had his client's consent to the wrongdoing, or he made full restitution to the injured parties. The only acceptable excuses (or at least the two defenses that are most likely to persuade the panel) are that the misconduct did not occur, or if it did, the attorney did not do it.

At the conclusion of the hearing, the panel must make a determination as to the merits of the claim. If it is satisfied that the attorney is blameless, or that there is insufficient evidence to support the charge of misconduct, the matter will be dismissed. On the other hand, if the panel is of the view that the attorney acted unethically, it can either refer the matter to the court for further action or end the case then and there by issuing a letter of admonition or caution. If it chooses the latter course of action, the attorney is getting off lightly. Letters of admonition or caution are confidential communications that act as a warning to the attorney to straighten out his behavior. These letters usually say little more than "Go forth and sin no more" and are generally not made available to the public. In some states, such letters do not even become part of the attorney's permanent record of discipline. The justification for this confidentiality is to protect an attorney's reputation from being tarnished by minor problems or innocent misunderstandings with clients that have now been worked out. (Either party's right to appeal at this juncture varies widely from state to state and, as a general proposition, favors the attorney and not the complainant.)

Where more serious concerns have been established, the grievance committee may elect to press formal charges and refer the matter to a court. At this point, the proceedings have been elevated out of the private arena of the bar association committee and into the public forum of the court system. A trial will be held with the grievance committee presenting evidence of misconduct and the attorney putting on a defense. At the conclusion of the trial, a decision will be rendered, which, in the majority of states, either party may appeal.

If the attorney is found guilty, the court has a variety of sanctions at its disposal. While the nomenclature varies from place to place, the range of punishment is as follows:

- *Censure:* This is a formal public statement that reprimands the attorney for violating ethical standards and that is published in legal newspapers and professional journals. While the lawyer's professional reputation is tarnished in the short run, the public at large generally does not get wind of the wrongdoing and the attorney is allowed to continue his practice.

- *Suspension:* Suspension can range from one day to several years. In the majority of states, there is no limit on the length of time an attorney can be suspended. Not only is this sanction a blow to the lawyer's reputation but it can also hurt his bank account if he is kept from his livelihood for very long. In some states, once the period of the suspension has passed, the attorney must apply for reinstatement. In other states, he is automatically entitled to pick up where he left off without having to prove that he turned over a new leaf in the interim. In almost every state, a lawyer who is suspended for more than six months must notify his clients and opposing counsel of his status.

- *Disbarment:* An attorney who is disbarred is no longer permitted to practice law, and his name is stricken from the roll of licensed attorneys. This is the harshest of all the penalties and, as such, is reserved for conduct that is criminal, borderline criminal, or grievous malpractice. In almost every state, an attorney who has been disbarred bears the obligation of informing his clients and opposing counsel.

The foregoing penalties represent the main categories of sanctions that a court is authorized to impose in disciplinary cases. In addition, and depending upon state law, a court may order a lawyer to make restitution to injured parties, contribute to the client security fund (discussed below), present proof that whatever problems caused him to be into trouble have been remedied, or seek psychiatric care. In some places (California, for example), lawyers who have been suspended are required to pass an ethics test before they will be reinstated. In every state, if the court concludes that the attorney acted illegally (as well as unethically), the case may be referred to the prosecuting attorney's office.

There are a couple of points worth noting before we leave this area of sanctions. The first is that most suspension and disbarment orders will be appealed by the attorney. There is nothing surprising in this, but what is noteworthy is that in over fifteen states, the attorney is allowed to continue to practice until all the appeals have been exhausted. Sometimes this can take years. (In some states, until the appeal has been concluded and absent a court order to the contrary, the attorney is not under an obligation to inform his clients of his status.) And even if the attorney loses the appeal, in forty-five states, he or she can still apply for reinstatement at some point in the future.

The second peculiarity you should recognize is that an attorney who is suspended or disbarred in one state, can pack up his books, move to another state, open an office, and resume business as usual. In an effort to cut down on this sort of thing, some states have enacted "reciprocal suspension or disbarment" laws, which prohibit an attorney from slipping out from under a penalty by crossing state lines.

The likelihood of discipline: Now that you understand the complaint process, you may wonder what the likelihood is that a complaint will result in discipline. Others—including the American Bar Association's Committee on Professional Responsibility and Standing Committee on Professional Discipline—have been wondering the same thing. Through the efforts of the ABA, the National Discipline Data Bank was established in 1968 to compile information on questions such as how many complaints are filed each year, what kinds of activities are complained of, what kinds of sanctions are imposed, what percentage of a state's bar association budget is dedicated to the enforcement of discipline, and how disciplinary procedures vary from state to state.

The National Discipline Data Bank has published numerous reports with the statistical information it has compiled. [Copies of the most current report, "Statistical Report Re: Public Discipline of Lawyers by Disciplinary Agencies, 1979–1983," are available for five dollars per copy from the American Bar Association, Order Fulfillment Department, 750 North Lake Shore Drive, Chicago, Illinois 60611; (312) 988-5000.] Due to the tremendous variation in disciplinary procedures from state to state and the fact that participation in the data bank surveys is voluntary (with some states declining to provide information), it is difficult, at this writing, to provide a national picture of the effectiveness of disciplinary enforcement efforts.

Apart from the ABA's effort to provide a big-picture, comparative analysis of the how and why of lawyer discipline, however, select individual states have been active in monitoring the activities and spending of their disciplinary committees. To give you a rough idea of what happens to the huge volume of complaints filed each year, let's consider the findings of two of the more diligent states—California and New York.

According to a background paper (dated June 1984) prepared by the State Bar of California, Office of Bar Communication and Public Affairs, there were approximately 84,000 attorneys in the state in 1983 and a total of 8,094 complaints, some of which were from a backlog from the year before. The majority of the complaints (7,139) were dispensed with during the initial screening phase and resulted in dismissals or postponements. Only 955 were more formally investigated. After a further filtering process, 17 resulted in admonishments, 29 ended in private censures, 17 resulted in public censures, 83 ended in suspensions, 13 resulted in disbarment, and in 9 cases, the attorneys were allowed to resign with charges pending.

The statistics for New York, published in the 1982 annual report of the Committee on Professional Discipline of the New York State Bar Association, cover complaints filed in 1982. (The figures for 1983 are not yet available.) A conservative estimate of the number of lawyers in the state during this year is 71,750. At the start of the year there were approximately 3,032 complaints pending, to which 8,178 new complaints were added. Again, the majority of the complaints (8,192) were dispensed with during the initial screening phase and resulted in dismissals, referrals to other agencies, cautionary letters, and other minor reprimands. A total of 573 were referred to the courts for further disposition and added to their backlog of 148 cases. At this point, all complaints dealing with a single lawyer were consolidated. Of the 211 disciplinary cases closed by the courts in 1982, there were 7 dismissals, 18 denials of reinstatement, 13 grants of reinstatement, 1 private censure, 16 public censures, 46 suspensions, 30 disbarments, and 67 other miscellaneous dispositions, and 13 attorneys were allowed to resign with the charges pending.

As is no doubt evident, the number of disciplinary complaints that result in serious penalties is very small indeed. And while these statistics are instructive, they still do not tell the whole story. There are undoubtedly many instances of misconduct that are never reported to the state disciplinary boards and, as such, are not reflected in the above tabulations. The fact that clients are the single largest group of persons to bring complaints serves to limit the kind and number of complaints brought to the attention of the disciplinary boards. Unless a problem tends to affect the client's personal interests, there is little incentive to bring a complaint. Few clients, for example, complain about an attorney's solicitation or wrongdoing that works to their advantage. Other forms of misconduct may be so subtle or technical that a client does not perceive them.

The best way for you to determine the likelihood that a complaint will result in disciplinary measures in your state is to look into the organization and operation of your local disciplinary board. Ask for a copy of their annual report, rules, regulations, and statistical analyses. From this material, you should be able to determine such factors as whether there are nonlawyers on the panel, whether there is a right of an appeal from any stage of the proceeding, if hearings are open to the complainant, whether arbitration of certain types of complaints is mandatory, whether there are public records of the proceedings, and whether there is adequate funding and sufficient staffing to process complaints in a timely manner. A grievance committee that lacks all or most of these essential features decreases the likelihood that your complaint will result in effective discipline.

Is it worth the effort? If the disciplinary system is as inadequate or lenient as some critics claim, the obvious next question is why bother to participate in it at all? The answer, quite simply, is that the consumer of legal services is ultimately the most effective regulator of the delivery of legal care in this country. Disciplinary committees can hardly be characterized as aggressive, and they depend upon consumer complaint to assist them in singling out the troublesome lawyers. Consumer complaint also serves to point the way to the areas of professional behavior in need of reform on a state and a national level.

Societal good aside for the moment, there is a more immediate benefit for the complainant as well. Though a disciplinary action will not usually result in the award of money or other tangible benefit, the complaint process will create an official record of discontent on the part of the client, which could be useful to support your side of the story in a fee dispute or subsequent malpractice suit.

MALPRACTICE

Unlike a disciplinary complaint, a successful malpractice suit can result in a dollar recovery to the client. Perhaps this reason, coupled with the ineffectiveness of the grievance route, has caused the number of malpractice suits to soar in recent years. Indeed, the situation has gotten out of control. The ABA's Standing Committee on Lawyer's Professional Liability reports that in 1950, only 5 percent of the practicing lawyers carried malpractice insurance. Today, in excess of 75 percent are insured.

Small wonder when you consider the kinds of bizarre cases brought against lawyers these days. One such case brought to my attention recently involved a client who was forced to change counsel in the middle of a case due to his first attorney's failing health. Unhappy with the result, he sued the first lawyer alleging that he should have taken better care of himself. Another extraordinary case involved a client who was referred to a specialist who, as luck would have it, turned out to be incompetent. Not only did the client sue the specialist, which might have been understandable, but stretching the point, he sued the referring lawyer as well.

The court system is by no means the panacea for every ill and annoyance. It should not be used to cover up one's own poor judgment or to shift responsibility onto someone else's shoulders. It is also no place to seek a fortune. If your complaint is really serious and you are unable to reach an agreement with the attorney as to how the matter may be resolved, a malpractice suit is certainly an alternative, but it should be considered a recourse of last resort.

Recognizing the wrong: One of the biggest stumbling blocks to bringing a malpractice suit is recognizing poor performance when you see it. There can be many forms of malpractice—inattentiveness, deceitfulness, and incompetence among them. Inattentiveness is not terribly difficult to spot. Missing deadlines, chronically running late, securing an inordinate number of extensions from the court or opposing counsel, glossing over details, and generally not pushing ahead on things are the most common forms. Similarly, most people can recognize deceitful behavior when they see it. Stealing money, lying or misrepresenting important facts, breaching a confidence, and withholding pertinent information necessary to make informed judgments about the case are examples of dishonest behavior. The real stickler comes in trying to recognize incompetence.

Everyone has a different understanding of incompetence. For purposes of our discussion here, I will define incompetence as the failure to perform adequately the services agreed upon at the start of the representation. This can encompass a multitude of sins. The failure of an attorney to know the law or to research what he doesn't understand, the failure to exercise sound judgment, the inability to develop careful strategies, the failure to compose sound arguments, and the failure to be intimately acquainted with every factual and legal principle involved in the matter are all examples of incompetence.

Even with a basic understanding of incompetence, however, the problem of course is that much of what a lawyer does for a living is out of the presence of the client. As a result, clients are often hard pressed to know what was done or not done in their case, or whether a judgment was hasty or well thought out but wrong. It is also extremely difficult for a client to distinguish between a bad case and a good case poorly handled. Without some technical expertise, it is quite difficult if not impossible in many cases to pinpoint acts of incompetent lawyering.

The requirement of damages: Assuming you are able to overcome the hurdle of recognizing the wrong, bear in mind that evidence of neglect, dishonesty, or incompetence alone is still not enough to give rise to a malpractice suit. The wrongful conduct must also have caused *damage* to you or your interests. Without specific, determinable damages, a malpractice claim will not lie.

The most common forms of malpractice: The American Bar Association and the major insurers of legal malpractice in this country joined forces in 1981 to create The National Legal Malpractice Data Center. Its mission is to compile data and conduct research on the increased incidence of malpractice claims in order to deal constructively with what appears to be an epidemic of lawsuits. Its findings, to date, provide us with a pretty good indication of the kinds of activities that clients feel warrant the institution of a malpractice claim. (Copies of the National Legal Malpractice Data Center publications can be obtained from the ABA Standing Committee on Professional Liability, 750 North Lake Shore Drive, Chicago, Illinois 60611; (312) 988-5755).

The Malpractice Data Center collected information on 18,420 malpractice claims filed from January 1, 1981, to September 30, 1983. From this analysis it concluded that the most predominant forms of malpractice occurred in four areas: the commingling of a client's funds either through negligence or intentional conduct, the failure to keep a client informed as to the progress of the case or to obtain his consent on important decisions, the missing of important deadlines such as allowing the statute of limitations to expire, and the failure to know and research substantive law.

Thanks to its research, we also know that over 80 percent of all malpractice claims filed in this country were against small firms numbering five attorneys or less and that roughly 52 percent of all malpractice claims arose out of errors associated with litigation. (It is interesting to note that generally 60 percent of all disciplinary complaints filed likewise stem from litigation. These numbers are high when you consider that litigation accounts for less than 20 percent of the national usage of lawyers.) The most troublesome subject matters have been real estate, personal injury (plaintiff's work), securities cases, bankruptcy, estates and trust work, and family law.

Who can sue? Contrary to popular belief, you do not have to be a client to have standing to sue an attorney for malpractice. Any person who claims to have been injured from the attorney's actions may initiate suit. Thus, for example, the beneficiaries of a negligently drawn will, the stockholders of a poorly negotiated corporate deal, or the grandparents on the losing side of a custody battle between a mother and a father may have standing to sue for malpractice. As a practical matter, however, roughly 87 percent of all malpractice claims are brought by clients.

On the subject of who can sue, bear in mind that of late, attorneys have been deciding to fight back. Lawyers (like doctors) are turning the tables by bringing countersuits for damages, which include a loss of income, loss of good standing in the community, and increases in insurance premiums. While the majority of such suits are designed to recoup losses, some attorneys are motivated out of a belief that many malpractice suits are brought simply to avoid the payment of attorney's fees. There is a high incidence of this, for example, in malpractice cases stemming out of family law. The Malpractice Data Center reports that 18 percent of such cases were filed after the attorney attempted to collect his fee. If enough attorneys elect to countersue, in time, this may put an end to such practices.

How long do you have? The question of how long you have before you must commence suit varies according to state law and the kind of malpractice alleged. Some years ago the rule was that a person had one to two years from the act that constituted malpractice within which suit had to be commenced. Today, many states have changed this rule to expand the statute of limitations. In these states, the clock does not begin to run until the discovery of the act or the start of the damage. For example, if an attorney was negligent in preparing a will for a client in 1965 and the client died in 1975, the beneficiaries who would be likely to complain of the malpractice, under the old rules, would have been barred from doing so. Under the new rules, the beneficiaries could bring suit if they did so within one to two years (depending upon state law) from the reading of the will.

As a practical matter, the National Legal Malpractice Data Center reports that close to half of all claims filed with insurance companies occur within one year from the alleged malpractice.

Finding representation: It is difficult to find a lawyer who is willing to sue a fellow lawyer for malpractice. This is all the more understandable when the lawyer you seek to sue is politically active in the bar or the community, is from a blue chip firm, or is widely regarded as a nice guy. There are some attorneys who specialize in these kinds of suits, however, and it would be worth your while to seek a specialist if you intend to try and beat a lawyer at his own game.

Collecting a judgment: If you win your suit, there is still the problem of collecting the judgment. Some lawyers do not carry malpractice insurance, and of the ones that do, the injury you claim may not be covered by the insurance policy. Typical exclusions, for example, include intentional torts; deceitful, malicious, fraudulent or criminal acts; claims based on actions by the attorney while he was acting in a nonlegal capacity, for example, as an officer or director of a corporation; bodily injury or loss of tangible property; punitive or exemplary damages; and securities violations. Don't underestimate the applicability of the latter—the state and federal securities laws have been held to apply to routine transactions such as the sale of a franchise, cooperative, condominium, or business.

If you are the victim of misappropriated funds, it might make much more sense to apply for reimbursement from the "client security fund" maintained by almost every state and many local bar associations. Client security funds are reserves of money set up to reimburse clients for losses from the dishonest (as opposed to negligent) conduct of a lawyer. They are funded from mandatory bar dues or by fee assessments imposed upon lawyers who are admitted to practice in the state, and they are administered by a trustee or a committee appointed by the bar association. Though it is often time-consuming to process a claim and while there is a maximum amount that can be recovered (usually from $10,000 to $50,000), if the attorney is insolvent, it does you little good to go through the time and expense of a court battle. If you are wondering about the likelihood of collecting from such a fund, call your local bar association and ask them for an application form as well as information on the average number and dollar amount of claims paid during the last year.

Is it worth the trouble? It is difficult to succeed in a malpractice suit. Not only do you have to spot the malpractice but you have to find a lawyer who will help you prove it and then try to collect a judgment. In the process, your private affairs will be paraded out into the open (remember that the "keeping confidences" rule is off when it comes to a malpractice suit), and you will have to bear the expense and aggravation of time-consuming litigation. It makes a lot more sense to try and work out an arrangement with the errant attorney before you go through the trouble of suing him. If the incidence of malpractice is obvious and the damage undeniable, the attorney will most likely be anxious to settle the matter before his or her reputation is put into jeopardy.

IN THE LAST ANALYSIS

It is possible to avoid the bother and aggravation associated with disciplinary actions and malpractice suits. The best and most assured way of accomplishing this, of course, is to find and work with competent counsel. They do exist and in fairly large numbers. Indeed, I have been privileged to know and work with a lot of capable, honest, and all-around splendid lawyers. My hope is that with the assistance of this book, you will be able to say the same.

Appendix

State Bar Associations

Alabama State Bar
415 Dexter Avenue
Post Office Box 671
Montgomery, Alabama 36106
(205) 269-1515

Alaska Bar Association
Post Office Box 279
Anchorage, Alaska 99510
(907) 272-7469

State Bar of Arizona
Suite 858
234 North Central
Phoenix, Arizona 85004
(602) 252-4804

Arkansas Bar Association
400 West Markham
Little Rock, Arkansas 72201
(501) 375-4605

State Bar of California
555 Franklin Street
San Francisco, California 94102
(415) 561-8200

Colorado Bar Association
Suite 800
250 West 14th Avenue
Denver, Colorado 80204
(303) 629-6873

Connecticut Bar Association
101 Corporate Place
Rocky Hill, Connecticut 06067
(203) 721-0025

Delaware State Bar Association
Carvel State Office Building
820 North French Street
Wilmington, Delaware 19801
(302) 658-5278

District of Columbia Bar
1426 H Street, N.W.
8th Floor
Washington, D.C. 20005
(202) 638-1500

Bar Association of the District of Columbia
Suite 300
1819 H Street, N.W.
Washington, D.C. 20006
(202) 223-1480

Florida Bar
Tallahassee, Florida 32301
(904) 222-5286

State Bar of Georgia
84 Peachtree Street
11th Floor
Atlanta, Georgia 30303
(404) 522-6255

Hawaii State Bar Association
820 Mililani
Post Office Box 26
Honolulu, Hawaii 96810
(808) 537-1868

Idaho State Bar
Post Office Box 895
Boise, Idaho 83701
(208) 342-8958

Illinois State Bar Association
Illinois Bar Center
Springfield, Illinois 62701
(217) 525-1760

Indiana State Bar Association
230 East Ohio Street
Sixth Floor
Indianapolis, Indiana 46204
(317) 639-5465

Iowa State Bar Association
1101 Fleming Building
Des Moines, Iowa 50309
(515) 243-3179

Kansas Bar Association
1200 Harrison Street
Post Office Box 1037
Topeka, Kansas 66601
(913) 234-5696

Kentucky Bar Association
West Main at Kentucky River
Frankfort, Kentucky 40601
(502) 564-3795

Louisiana State Bar Association
Suite 600
210 O'Keefe Avenue
New Orleans, Louisiana 70112
(504) 566-1600

Maine State Bar Association
124 State Street
Post Office Box 788
Augusta, Maine 04330
(207) 622-7523

Maryland State Bar Association, Inc.
Suite 905
207 East Redwood Street
Baltimore, Maryland 21202
(301) 685-7878

Massachusetts Bar Association
One Center Plaza
Boston, Massachusetts 02108
(617) 523-4529

State Bar of Michigan
306 Townsend Street
Lansing, Michigan 48933
(517) 372-9030

Minnesota State Bar Association
Suite 403
430 Marquette Avenue
Minneapolis, Minnesota 55401
(612) 333-1183

Mississippi State Bar
Post Office Box 2168
Jackson, Mississippi 39205
(601) 948-4471

The Missouri Bar
Post Office Box 119
Jefferson City, Missouri 65102
(314) 635-4128

State Bar of Montana
Post Office Box 4669
Helena, Montana 59604
(406) 442-7660

Nebraska State Bar Association
1019 American Charter Center
206 South 13th Street
Lincoln, Nebraska 68508
(402) 475-7091

State Bar of Nevada
834 Willow Street
Reno, Nevada 89502
(702) 329-4100

New Hampshire Bar Association
18 Centre Street
Concord, New Hampshire 03301
(603) 224-6942

New Jersey State Bar Association
172 West State Street
Trenton, New Jersey 08608
(609) 394-1101

State Bar of New Mexico
1117 Stanford Avenue, N.E.
Post Office Box 25883
Albuquerque, New Mexico 87125
(505) 842-6132

New York State Bar Association
One Elk Street
Albany, New York 12207
(518) 463-3200

North Carolina State Bar
Post Office Box 25908
Raleigh, North Carolina 27611
(919) 828-4620

North Carolina Bar Association
1025 Wade Avenue
Post Office Box 12806
Raleigh, North Carolina 27605
(919) 828-0561

State Bar Association of North Dakota
Post Office Box 2136
Bismarck, North Dakota 27605
(701) 255-1404

Ohio State Bar Association
33 West 11th Avenue
Columbus, Ohio 43201
(614) 421-2121

Oklahoma Bar Association
Post Office Box 53036
Oklahoma City, Oklahoma 73152
(405) 524-2365

Oregon State Bar
1776 S.W. Madison Street
Portland, Oregon 97205
(503) 224-4280

Pennsylvania Bar Association
100 South Street
Post Office Box 186
Harrisburg, Pennsylvania 17108
(717) 238-6715

Puerto Rico Bar Association
Post Office Box 1900
San Juan, Puerto Rico 00903
(809) 721-3358

Rhode Island Bar Association Offices
1804 Industrial Bank Building
Providence, Rhode Island 02903
(401) 421-5740

South Carolina Bar
Post Office Box 11039
Columbia, South Carolina 29211
(803) 799-6653

State Bar of South Dakota
222 East Capitol
Pierre, South Dakota 57501
(605) 224-7554

Tennessee Bar Association
3622 West End Avenue
Nashville, Tennessee 37205
(615) 383-7421

State Bar of Texas
Post Office Box 12487
Austin, Texas 78711
(512) 475-4200

Utah State Bar
425 East 100 South
Salt Lake City, Utah 84111
(801) 531-9077

Vermont Bar Association
Post Office Box 100
Montpelier, Vermont 05602
(802) 223-2020

Virginia State Bar
Suite 1622, 700 Building
Richmond, Virginia 23219
(804) 786-2061

Virginia Bar Association
Suite 708
701 East Franklin Street
Charlottesville, Virginia 23219
(804) 644-0041

Washington State Bar Association
505 Madison Street
Seattle, Washington 98104
(206) 622-6054

West Virginia State Bar
E-400 State Capitol
Charleston, West Virginia 25305
(304) 346-8414

West Virginia Bar Association
Post Office Box 346
Charleston, West Virginia 25322
(304) 342-1474

State Bar of Wisconsin
Post Office Box 7158
Madison, Wisconsin 53707
(608) 257-3838

Wyoming State Bar
Post Office Box 109
Cheyenne, Wyoming 82003
(307) 632-9061

Index

INDEX